The Immigrant's Guide to Living in

Australia

3rd Edition
Revised, Improved and Expanded

Hymie Zaw

NOTE:

This is a guide. It is not a substitute for obtaining legal advice about your lease, finances or taxation. Nor is it a replacement for a qualified financial advisor. You are encouraged to seek such legal and financial advice where necessary.

DISCLAIMER

At the time of going to press, all information in this book was accurate as the author was able to ascertain within reason. All references to private or state organisations are gratuitous. The author has no financial interest in them and does nor stand to benefit from them in any way

Veritax Business Consultants Pty Ltd

16 Eildon Street

Doncaster Vic 3108

Australia

WEBSITE: www.placeofbooks.com

Cover Design and typeset by BookPOD

Cover Image: iStockphoto

ISBN: 978-0-9873302-9-1 (pbk)

eISBN: 978-0-9945532-0-1 (ebook)

A Catalogue-in-Publication is available from the National Library of Australia.

Biography

Hymie Zawatzky understands what it means to be an immigrant – to leave one's homeland and embark on a journey to an unknown destination. He and his wife arrived in Australia from South Africa in 1979 and settled in Melbourne. He is the son of immigrant parents who left Europe in the 1920s for South Africa. As a qualified and experienced chartered accountant (FCPA) he was able to establish himself in Australia. Later he moved on to start his own consulting company specialising in the retail and property industry.

The process of immigration and assisting new migrants is one of his special interests. This led him to serve on the steering committee of the Ethnic Council of Victoria and to establish a new ethnic radio station in Victoria. Presently nearly every ethnic group broadcasts on radio.

He is the author of *Australia the Immigrant's Guide to Retail, Retail Survival in Tough Time* and *The Retailers' Guide to Lease Negotiation and Administration,* all of which are available for review on his web site www.placeofbooks.com.

His practical and theoretical understanding of Australian finance, his own experience in immigrating, plus a great deal of research, has given him an ideal background to writing this book.

Author's note

Since the second edition of this book, there have been a number of important changes in Australian life, which will have an impact on any new migrant. This has motivated me to provide new migrants with the following additional assistance found in this 2016 revised and expanded Third Edition.

- The changes in the economy. The Australian dollar is presently worth less and buys less.
- The latest guide to house and apartment prices in major cities.
- A current guide to the cost of renting houses and apartments.
- The changes in the cost of private schooling fees.
- Alterations to family benefits.
- The updated salary structure in Australia
- The changes in income tax and its impact on new migrants.
- Recommended high performing schools in major cities.
- All a migrant needs know about going into a retail business.
- The "do's" and "don'ts" about entering into an Australian franchise operation.
- More about the Australian lifestyle and customs, to help a migrant integrate into Australian society.
- The many benefits available to migrants with the "senior card", available to all Australians over sixty.
- The low cost assistance provided by municipal councils. This is particularly valuable to migrants who bring elderly parents with them to Australia.
- New Australian citizenship rights for New Zealanders living in Australia.

I hope that this book will be of assistance to all new migrants and their families, as well as to people considering coming to Australia.

The very best of luck to you and your family.

Hymie Zawatzky
Melbourne

This book is dedicated

to my wife, Joan.

I thank my

parents Ken and Bashke

for having the courage to

emigrate to a new country.

Contents

1

Your Decision

Welcome,

Once you have made the decision to emigrate to Australia, and have your permanent residence visa and air tickets, you will have a number of questions. This book has been written to help answer most of your questions, and act as a guide during your first few years in Australia.

These are some of the questions you may ask:

- What do I take with me on the plane?
- Who will meet me at the airport?
- How do I transport my luggage from the airport to my first night's lodgings?
- Where do I stay until I am ready to rent a house or apartment on a more permanent basis?
- What should I look out for when renting a home or apartment?
- What is the cost of renting a house or apartment in Melbourne, Sydney or Perth?
- Once I have found a home to rent, how do I organise telephones, electricity, gas and other important connections.
- Will it be easy to settle in to my new home?
- What are the real estate prices in Melbourne and Sydney?
- How do I go about buying my first home and what traps should I avoid?

- Should I bring a car with me to Australia or buy one when I arrive?
- Is public transport available?
- What is the salary structure in Australia compared to my home country?
- How do I go about finding a job?
- I am a qualified professional. What will I have to do to convert my qualification to an Australian qualification?
- I have a trade. What wage can I expect in Australia?
- What is the status of women in Australian society?
- I am pregnant and if my child is born in Australia, how do I register the birth?
- How will I find a job, and will I be entitled to claim any unemployment benefits?
- How long will it take me to become an Australian citizen?
- Will I have to undergo military service in Australia?
- How does the Australian taxation system operate?
- How does the banking system work, and how do I get an introduction to a bank?
- How do prices of goods in Australia compare with those in my home country?
- If both parents work, are there suitable child care facilities in Australia?
- What is the cost of education in Australia? Can I send my child to a private school if I have the means?
- Are family allowances available to assist me in supporting and educating my children?
- When I arrive, how will I go about finding a new doctor, lawyer, pharmacist or accountant?
- With the high cost of medical care today, is there a national health scheme in existence?

- My parents are coming with me, will they be entitled to benefits or be able to claim the old-age pension? If I have a pension from my home country can I transfer it to Australia?
- What is the Australian lifestyle?
- What is the Australian attitude to household pets?
- What is the cost of petrol, and is it expensive to get around such a large country as Australia?
- How will I, as a new immigrant, be able to maintain my cultural and religious links with the 'old country'?
- I am a member of Rotary International. Are there similar service clubs in Australia?
- How do I go about buying a franchise?
- I'm from New Zealand. How do I settle in Australia?

Moving to a new country is not easy as you are confronted with a lot of new laws, rules, values and attitudes. Read this book slowly and carefully and by the time you have finished it, you will have a far better idea of what your life and your family's lives will be like in Australia.

Not only will you find answers to these questions throughout the book, but you may have some of your own. Thinking through the questions and answers systematically, will I am sure, help smooth the way for you as you start out on your new life in Australia, and help you to settle soon and successfully.

2

What to take with you on the plane

Your luggage

Most international airlines allow each passenger only one large suitcase in the hold of the aircraft and one item of hand luggage, plus a coat in the cabin. This does limit the personal effects that immigrants can bring along on the plane.

To compensate for this, you should think about sending unaccompanied luggage a week or so ahead of your journey, or on the same plane with you. In this way, you will at least have some of your essential possessions until your 'lift' or container arrives by boat.

The 'lift' may take as long as six weeks to arrive in Australia, and strikes could lengthen this period. This means carefully planning what to take in your luggage.

The final composition of your luggage will depend on where you are settling in Australia, and whether you are arriving in summer or winter. Be sure to check climatic conditions for the area where you have chosen to settle.

To help you, I have compiled a list of items, based upon my own experience, which I believe you should pack in your luggage:

Adults

- One long sleeve and two sleeveless 'singlets' (vests) for men and spencers for ladies, and the equivalent for children.

- One suit and one sports coat plus flannels and the equivalent for ladies, suitable for job interviews.
- Walking shoes or sneakers for each person in your group and one smart pair of shoes for each adult.
- A warm sweater/jacket for each person.
- If you are arriving in spring, winter or autumn, a track suit or leisure garment for each member of the family.
- A towel for each person.
- A small supply of essential family medicines, as the trade names and formulations you are used to may be different in Australia.
- A short medical summary in English for each family member and the medications they are taking, even if they have other generic names in your country of origin.
- A 'doona' (duvet, featherbed), cover or sleeping bag, for each member of the family (this might be packed in your unaccompanied luggage).
- An umbrella.
- A good pocket knife with an attached can opener, corkscrew and blade (placed in your main baggage not cabin luggage).
- A document case for all your essential papers: birth and professional certificates, employment resumes, medical records, references and other key identification documents.
- An international driver's licence.
- An international credit card, if you have one.

Infants

Travelling long distances with infants and small children can be very trying, but you can make things a lot more comfortable for them and for yourself by having easy access to these essentials:

- A big carrier bag for all the following bits and pieces – preferably one with lots of compartments for separating the soiled from the clean.
- Disposable nappies and cleansing equipment.
- Sterilised bottles for milk and other fluids as children easily become dehydrated on the aeroplane.
- Two complete changes of clothing - an all-in-one outer garment, bootees and a 'sweater' (jersey/jumper).
- Two light wrapping blankets (in case one becomes soiled).
- Garbage bags (for soiled clothing).
- Feeding bibs.
- Towelets and tissues.
- Paracetamol, gripe water and an anti-spasmodic (there's nothing worse than a distressed child in the confines of an aircraft!)
- Baby foods, preferably in jars - enough for the entire journey and for at least the first three meals in Australia, as well as for any unexpected airline delays.
- A carrying crib.

Hints

- Some people ask their family doctor to recommend a mild sedative for the flight.

- Some children experience severe earache during take-off and landing if their ears are blocked. Providing them with a sweet or with something suitable to suck during this time may be helpful. If your infant or toddler has a cold, a stuffy nose or any sort of ear infection, remember to ask your doctor for something to assist the condition.

Toddlers and children

- At least one complete change of outer clothing, and two of underclothing.
- A 'sweater' (jumper/jersey).
- Towelets and a face-cloth.
- Paracetamol.
- Games, books and comics.

Hints

If you are traveling with small children, you should try to book the aircraft early, and ask if you can have adequate space for your child to lie down. The bulkhead, with its extra floor space, is the ideal position, and if the plane is not too full, booking/check in staff will always do their best to oblige you.

3

Arriving at the airport and your first night's lodgings

When you arrive in Australia

As you step off the plane, your immediate priority is how to get your family and luggage to your accommodation. If you have not made arrangements for accommodation you will be assisted with a hotel booking at the airport.

One of the first things you will have to do is to clear customs.

After that, you may want to exchange traveller's cheques into Australian currency. Australian currency is decimal. Notes are in $100, $50, $20, $10, and $5 denominations. Coins are in 5c, 10c, 50c, $1 and $2. Exchange facilities are available at all incoming airports. Most banks will also exchange traveller's cheques

Goods brought into Australia may require the payment of customs duty and sales tax. However, travellers are allowed to bring certain goods into Australia duty and sales tax free. Check with your travel agent, before embarking as to what is allowed as it is constantly changing.

Like most immigrants, you will probably have parcels, hand luggage, coats, and as many suitcases as the airline allows you to take on board. You may also have sent unaccompanied luggage to meet you on arrival, but this can be collected at a later date. Remember, unaccompanied luggage does not enjoy sales tax and customs duty concessions

If possible, try to arrange for a friend or relative to meet you at the airport. Remember, the friend may have work commitments, so try to arrange arrival at your final destination on a weekend, or after 5 pm on a working day.

If you can get *two* friends, with *two* cars, then so much the better. The boot of a car has its limitations (unless your friend has a van or SUV) and you may still have to hire a taxi if you need additional space.

Most taxis have limited luggage space, so the trip could be rather costly. You should expect to pay at least $70 from the airport to your destination. Ensure that you have cash readily available before you take the taxi.

An alternative, is to take an airport bus to the city terminal. However, this means you still have to get from the terminal to the place where you have booked to stay for that first night.

Car Hire

You may have planned to stop off elsewhere in Australia for a few days, prior to arriving to the city where you have decided to begin your new life. In this case, consider hiring a car to await you at the airport for use over this period. On a daily basis, cars cost about the same as a cab fare, but offer greater independence.

When you arrive at your final point of destination, you might feel more relaxed if you have transport of your own for the first few days. You could take advantage of special weekend and other hire rates offered by companies like Hertz, Avis, Budget or Thrifty. These car hire companies all have counters at the airport. They also supply you with adequate maps for ease of navigation. Though car hire is a costly way of getting around, it provides independence and could save you from a lot of stressful decision-making.

Street Directories

The acquisition of a street directory is a must immediately on your arrival. These are very accurate, detailed and absolutely indispensable if you want to feel comfortable in your new homeland.

The following are the names of the standard street directories: U.B.D., Melways or Gregory's.

Car hire companies in the major cities will usually include a copy of the relevant street directory in your rented vehicle. The directories can be purchased at many newsagents or automobile club stores

Most airports are about 25 minutes' drive to the city and roads are well signposted, so driving into town should not be too difficult. If you arrive after 5 pm on weekdays or over weekends you are unlikely to hit peak hour traffic.

An international driving licence is acceptable to all car hire companies, so ensure that you have one before leaving for Australia.

Hints on Road Travel

- In Australia, we drive on the left hand side of the road and the person on the driver's right usually has the right of way.

- Trams and buses have right of way, so stop when they stop.

- It would be helpful if a friend or relative could buy you the standard booklet of road signs and driving in Australia. This only costs a few dollars and contains all the questions that you will have to answer to convert your international licence to an Australian one.

If you can present an international licence from your home country you will only have to sit a short written test and do not have to repeat the practical driving test.

11

It is important to note that in Australia your driver's licence which includes your photograph is one of the most important documents you will need to identify yourself.

4

Where to stay until you are ready to rent a house or apartment

A place to stay

The most pressing task facing many new arrivals is to find a place to stay for the first week or ten days, until they find a house or apartment to rent.

The most fortunate situation would be if you have friends or relatives who can provide accommodation for you. They will also be able to advise you on the do's and don'ts of renting your own home.

Your hosts will introduce you to the local customs, style of shopping, prices of goods and commodities, and generally how the typical Australian household is organised.

Most Australian households do not have full-time domestic help and each member of the home has to do their share of the housework. As a temporary family member your help with household chores will be expected.

If you and your family need to stay in a hotel or motel, I advise against staying in the normal business or tourist hotels in the centre of the city. These are very expensive; for a family of four you could pay as much as $1800 a week.

5

The cost of renting a house or apartment in major Australian cities

To give you an idea of rentals in a major city in Australia, I have chosen Melbourne, Sydney and Brisbane as examples.

Melbourne

The major source of statistics for this report is the Domain Group and the Department of Health and Human services Rental Report).

When you rent a property in Melbourne, you will be required to lodge a bond as security which is refunded to you when you leave the property at the end of your lease term. The bond is usually equal to a month's rent plus one month's rent in advance.

In metropolitan Melbourne, median rents averaged from $330 per week in the Western Melbourne region to $425 for the inner Melbourne region. Houses tend to be the dominant rental property in outer metropolitan areas, whereas apartments are more prevalent in areas closer to the centre of Melbourne.

The following is a table of rents by statistical region in Metropolitan Melbourne.

Inner Melbourne	$425
Inner Eastern Melbourne	$400
Southern Melbourne	$405

Western Melbourne	$330
North Western Melbourne	$350
North Eastern Melbourne	$350
Outer Eastern Melbourne	$360
South Eastern Melbourne	$330
Mornington Peninsula	$330

The following table lists medium rents by major property type in Metropolitan Melbourne and Regional Victoria for the June 2015 quarter

	Metropolitan	Regional
1 Bedroom apartment	$315	$175
2 Bedroom apartment	$390	$230
3 Bedroom apartment	$420	$300
2 Bedroom House	$400	$240
3 Bedroom House	$360	$285
4 Bedroom House	$420	$350

The location of the property determines the rental per week. The better the location the higher the rent per week.

If we look at a 2 bedroom apartment, the following are the highest and lowest medium rentals in Melbourne:-

Highest	
Docklands	$558
Port Melbourne	$570
Southbank	$550
Fitzroy	$530
CBD – St Kilda Rd	$525
Balwyn	$588

Lowest	
Melton	$240
Werribee	$260
Dromana/Portsea	$265

If we look at a 3 bedroom house the following are the highest and lowest median rentals per suburbs:-

Highest	
Toorak	$1,020
East Melbourne	$948
Armadale	$870
Albert Park	$800
Brighton	$800
Lowest	
Melton	$275
Werribee	$300
Pakenham	$300
St Albans	$310

Sydney

The following table lists medium rents by major property type in greater Sydney:

Metropolitan	Inner Ring	Middle Ring	Outer Ring	Rest
1 Bedroom apartment	$510	$460	$340	$240
2 Bedroom apartment	$480	$480	$400	$320
2 Bedroom House	$670	$460	$358	$340
3 Bedroom House	$850	$550	$430	$380

If we look at a 2 bedroom apartment, the following are the highest and lowest medium rentals in Sydney by suburb:

Highest	
Leichardt	$650
North Sydney	$650
Sydney	$720
Waverley	$680
Woollahra	$700
Manly	$730
Lowest	
Fairfield	$330
Gosford	$350
Hawkesbury	$320
Penrith	$310
Wyong	$310
Blue Mountains	$350

If we look at a 3 bedroom house the following are the highest and lowest median rentals:

Highest	
Waverley	$1100
North Sydney	$1100
Woollahra	$1100
Manly	$1000
Sydney	$880
Lane Cove	$875
Randwick	$870
Lowest	
Cessnock	$300

Wyong	$380
Port Stephens	$350
Maitland	$340
Blue Mountains	$400
Campbelltown	$400
Shellharbour	$370

Brisbane

The average median rent in Brisbane city for a 2 bedroom apartment is $380 per week, which is much lower than Sydney, but slightly higher than Melbourne.

The following is a selection of property by type for Brisbane:

Metropolitan	
1 Bedroom apartment	$355
2 Bedroom apartment	$380
3 Bedroom apartment	$410
3 Bedroom House	$390
4 Bedroom House	$430
5 Bedroom House	$620

If we look at a 2 bedroom apartment the following is a selection of medium rentals in Brisbane by suburb:

Caboolture	$298
Inner Brisbane	$475
Ipswich	$285
Logan City	$300
Northwest Inner Brisbane	$400
Redcliffe	$340

Redland City	$378
South East Inner	$400
South East Outer	$395

If we look at a 3 bedroom house the following is a selection of median rentals by suburb:

Caboolture	$345
Inner Brisbane	$550
Ipswich City	$340
Logan City	$380
Northwest Inner Brisbane	$500
Northwest Outer Brisbane	$420
Pine Rivers	$410
Redcliffe	$370
Redland City	$445
South East Inner Brisbane	$485
South East Outer Brisbane	$440

6

What should you look out for when renting a home or apartment

A permanent home

As soon as you have moved into your temporary accommodation, you may begin to think about finding a more permanent home. I suggest that you get to know your city first before deciding to buy a house or apartment.

Buying a house is an expensive exercise and you should make your decision only after much research and careful thought.

However, armed with a street directory, the advice of friends and family, and the property pages of the local newspapers, you will soon have a good idea of the area that will suit you best.

You will also have to wait until you have a settled job and can assure a bank of your ability to repay a mortgage.

To assist you, here are some aspects that you should bear in mind when trying to make your choice:

- Price per week you can afford to pay.
- Distance from the centre of the city.
- Distance from proposed schools for your children.
- Access to public transport.

- Whether you prefer older, inner suburbs or more modern outer areas.
- The quality, style and size of the home required.
- The distance to friends or relatives.
- Whether you wish to live in an area preferred by members of your ethnic or religious group?

Property Advertising in Newspapers

Having selected the areas in which you think you might like to live, you should make use of the newspapers that carry the bulk of advertisements for homes to let. These include the Saturday editions of *The Advertiser* in Adelaide, *The Age* in Melbourne, *The Sydney Morning Herald* in Sydney, or *The Courier Mail* in Brisbane. A number of computer sites like REA and others operated by real estate agents also give details of homes and apartments to let.

Many accommodation advertisements use abbreviations, which if you understand them, can save you unnecessary visits. Here are some of the more common terms:

4/5 Bedrm	=	4 bedrooms and study
AGPool	=	Above ground pool
BIR	=	built in wardrobes
BV	=	brick veneer
DH	=	ducted heating
IGPool	=	In ground pool
LU/Garage	=	lockup garage
Mod.Kit.	=	modern kitchen
WB	=	weatherboard (wood)
WI Pantry	=	walk in pantry
WWCarps	=	wall-to-wall carpets

Let's assume that you select the Doncaster/Templestowe area in Melbourne as a place where you might like to live. You will find several property agencies advertising for these areas, and most of them are situated close to each other, so you can comfortably call on all of them to discuss your needs.

If you want to rent rather than to buy, it is unlikely that an agent will go with you to view the property. You will simply be given the keys and charged a deposit which will be refunded on return of the keys.

Having found a home to rent, remember that both you and your landlord are bound by clearly specified rights and responsibilities. These are contained in a written lease and backed up by State Retail Tenancy Legislation.

Tenancy law is complicated and varies from state to state, so if you strike trouble with your landlord you can always get legal advice or help from a Tenant's Advisory Service.

The following are some of the essential points to bear in mind when renting a home:

Leases

You are best protected by a written lease, so avoid verbal lease agreements. Never sign a lease unless you have read it carefully and understood it, even if it appears to be in a standard printed format.

Do not be afraid to ask questions if you are not sure.

Bond Money

Most lease agreements include the payment of bond money, a sum equal to about a month's rent. Bond money acts as a guarantee against damage, unpaid rent and so on. It is paid in advance and in addition to your first week's rental. Make sure you receive a receipt for your bond money.

Before you move in, make a list of anything broken or damaged so that you cannot be held responsible for damage you did not cause. Also ensure that the agent or the owner signs the list.

When you move out, the bond money is refunded to you if you have fulfilled your side of the lease agreement.

In many of the states in Australia there is a statutory authority, such as a Rental Bond Board, to which all bond money is paid and which lays down clear procedures for its return.

Rent

The following points are worth noting:

- In Australia rent is usually paid weekly, unless some other arrangement is made with the landlord and written into the lease.
- The landlord or his agent may only vary the rental by agreement, with you or provided certain notice is given.
- Rent cannot be increased more than once in six months.
- A tenant may not withhold rent to force a landlord to carry out repairs.

Ending the Tenancy

If you want to end the tenancy:

- You have to give notice as contained in the lease.
- You can end your tenancy even if the lease is not up, but you will probably have to assist your landlord in finding a new tenant. This may mean that you will have to contribute to the cost of advertising for a new tenant.
- If a new tenant cannot be found, you may have to pay the rent to the end of the lease.
- To avoid such extra costs, you should carefully consider the length of the lease you require.

Eviction

A landlord cannot evict you without following these procedures:

He has to give you notice as laid down in the Residential Tenancies Act. In most cases the landlord must also get a court order for your eviction. If this happens, the court will usually give you time to find other accommodation.

- Even if the tenancy period ends, the landlord cannot just throw you out. He must give you notice and follow the proper legal procedures.
- The landlord cannot seize the tenant's furniture or other goods as compensation for rent owing.
- Of course, the landlord is ultimately entitled to his property back in good condition.

Repairs

- The landlord must ensure that the premises are fit to live in and in good repair.
- Depending on the terms of the lease, the landlord is responsible for carrying out all reasonable repairs, excluding damage caused by you.
- You are expected to take proper care of the premises and must pay for any damage you do to the property.
- You must not install any additional fixtures without the landlord's permission.

Privacy

Australians zealously guard their privacy.

- You are entitled to privacy in your own home and your landlord may only enter under conditions specified in your lease, and under the tenancy laws of the state.
- A landlord is usually required to give you notice before entering or inspecting the property.

7

Organising telephone, gas and electricity once you have found a home to rent

Most houses and apartments usually require only three services in order to be habitable - electricity, gas and telephone.

Power is easy to arrange. A telephone call to the State Electricity Commission and the Gas &Fuel Corporation will get things going very quickly.

Telephone lines and plugs are already installed in most homes in major cities. A call to your nearest Telecom office will ensure connection within about a week. There is a lot of competition for providing telephone services and you should ring around before making a commitment.

Many telephone companies offer packages covering land lines, mobile phones and internet services in one charge out rate. Be careful on how long you want to have your contract with the Telco as it is often difficult to change if you get a better deal from another company.

When arranging for connections with any of the public utilities, be sure to ask them to read the meters the day before you move in. This will ensure that you are not held responsible for the previous tenant's charges.

8

Settling in to your new home

If your furniture has not arrived in Australia before you move into your rented home, you must notify your clearing agent of your new address. This means that when your "lift" does arrive, the documents will reach you directly, and your goods can be cleared and delivered immediately. In this way you will avoid incurring demurrage charges.

Until your own household equipment arrives, you may need some basics to tide you over. The Yellow Pages directory available at post offices, provides lists of companies specialising in furniture hire. This service is not expensive if you are prepared to make do with essential furniture for a while.

Borrow crockery from friends, neighbours and relatives who are bound to have extra.

Some churches and community centres offer migrants assistance, so make yourself known to these organisations in your area. In this way you will also begin to establish yourself in your new community.

One of the most important things to do when you move into your home is to introduce yourself to your neighbours. If you are able to form a good relationship with your neighbours, they are likely to be a great help to you in the future.

Your neighbours will be able to advise you of all the council services and the amenities in your area, such as:

- The most convenient bus, tram and train connections.
- The nearest convenience store (general supply store) and shops.
- Council rules and regulations for things like burning of rubbish, control of dogs and cutting the grass on the sidewalk outside your home.
- When garbage is collected by the council.
- The local newsagent, so that you can have your newspaper delivered, if you wish.
- The nearest pharmacy.
- Where to find the nearest post office.
- Where to go to vote in municipal elections.
- Whether your suburb is part of Neighbourhood Watch (an informal neighbourhood security network) and who your contact person is.
- Where the nearest police station is to be found.
- The closest hospital

9

The real estate prices in Melbourne and Sydney

To give you a basic idea of real estate prices in Australia, I have accessed information on two of the major cities in Australia, namely Melbourne and Sydney.

A good source of information for new migrants is the real estate institutes in the various states. They publish the latest statistics on the sale of houses and apartments in those states.

The median price

House prices are usually measured by the *"median price"* for each suburb. The median is the middle price in a series of sales, where half of the sales are of lower value and half are of a higher value. For example if 15 sales are recorded in a suburb and arranged in order from the lowest to the highest value, the eighth sales price is the median price.

Median prices are used rather than average or mean price as they are then unaffected by a few unusually high or low prices in a series. Usually the median presents a more accurate indicator of true market activity.

Melbourne, Victoria

The Real Estate Institute of Victoria (REIV) September 2015 quarter medians show that the residential housing market in Melbourne continues to grow rapidly with a median house price in Melbourne of $729,500.

The median prices for apartments have also grown rapidly to $532,000.

An analysis by location shows the following median prices:-

	House	Apartment
Inner	$1,236,000	$560,000
Middle	$861,000	$586,500
Outer	$550,000	$415,500

The REIV recorded the median house and apartment prices for the following popular suburbs in Melbourne for the September 2015 quarter:

Suburb	House	Apartment
Brighton	$2,222,500	$920,000
Invanhoe	$1,330,000	$648,500
Toorak	$3,950,000	$1,001,000
Northcote	$1,138,900	$585,000
Footscray	$780,000	$367,500
Hawthorn	$2,053,000	$557,250
Doncaster East	$1,232,000	$740,000
Noble Park	$552,000	$349,500
Kew	$2,080,000	$649,500
Boronia	$620,000	$445,000
Keilor East	$740,000	$545,000
Balwyn	$2,281,000	$781,000
Box Hill	$1,574,000	$556,000
Caulfield North	$1,841,000	$693,000
Caulfield South	$1,235,000	$697,500
Doncaster	$1,298,000	$610,000
Flemington	$823,000	$402,750
Glen Waverley	$1,319,000	$870,500

Invanhoe	$1,330,000	$648,500
Lillidale	$577,500	$391,000
Malvern	$1,985,000	$755,444
North Melbourne	$1,065,000	$498,750
Nunawading	$892,500	$650,000
Port Melbourne	$1,305,000	$804,000
Preston	$815,000	$478,750
Ringwood	$850,000	$465,000
Richmond	$1,102,000	$520,000
Camberwell	$1,883,000	$811,750

Mortgage loans

Generally, in Australia, new borrowers currently can expect to pay about 4% – 6% interest on their mortgage loans, but this can vary considerably from bank to bank. Interest rates are established against the availability of funds and the current rates for deposits being paid.

Sydney

Sydney is a very widely spread out city divided into two distinct sectors separated by the Sydney Harbour Bridge.

New immigrant families tend to look for homes that are close to the schools they wish their children to attend.

Parents may want to send their children to a school catering to members of their own religious group. For example, Catholic parents might choose the eastern suburbs of Bondi, Bellevue Hill, Rose Bay, Bronte and Waverley. These are all areas in which they will find Catholic schools.

To give another example, Jewish parents wanting their children to attend a Jewish school on the North Shore, will try to buy a home in suburbs such as Killara, Lindfield and Pymble.

Housing Prices in Sydney

Sydney housing prices are probably the highest in Australia. As a guide, the following price listing was reported by Retail Estate View for the quarter ending June 2015. As explained previously, the median prices have been used as a basis.

The median price for houses for Sydney is $1,000,616 with apartments at $650,078. However if you want to live close to the city the prices will vary considerably. The distances are expressed in terms of "the inner ring."

The following is a selection of median prices in suburbs found to be popular with migrants with varying amounts of capital to invest in a house or apartment (sorted alphabetically):

Suburb	House	Apartment
Armidale	$340,000	$220,000
Bondi	$2,670,000	$925,000
Bondi Beach	$2,200,000	$925,000
Blacktown	$662,000	$446,000
Campbelltown	$530,000	$400,000
Chatswood	$2,439,000	$865,000
Coogee	$2,610,000	$850,000
Cronulla	$1,630,000	$685,000
Dover Heights	$3,272,500	$680,500
Fairfield	$730,000	$405,000
Glebe	$1,607,500	$865,000
Homebush	$1,825,000	$682,500
Hornsby	$1,227,500	$646,300
Hurtsville	$1,300,000	$720,000
Killara	$2,071,000	$ 1,142,000
Lane Cove	$2,800,000	$740,000

Lindfield	$2,180,000	$880,000
Liverpool	$742,500	$400,000
Marrickville	$1,213,500	$615,000
Miranda	$1,103,750	$630,000
Mosman	$3,250,000	$834,167
North Sydney	$1,786,000	$841,000
Parramatta	$1,345,500	$567,500
Penrith	$615,000	$355,000
Pymble	$2,020,000	$870,000
Randwick	$1,675,000	$868,750
Rose Bay	$3,135,000	$910,000
Ryde	$1,340,000	$691,000
St Ives	$1,694,000	$765,000
Strathfield	$2,275,500	$725,000
Sutherland	$845,500	$583,500
Vaucluse	$3,890,000	$1,030,000
Waverley	$1,900,000	$925,100
Willoughby	$1,716,000	$900,000

Median prices in rural towns of New South Wales

Some of the larger rural towns in New South Wales may be of interest to new migrants and the following are median prices:

Rural Town	House	Apartment
Bathurst	$349,000	$230,000
Coffs Harbour	$389,750	$252,500
Orange	$348,000	$225,000
Dubbo	$317,000	$297,500
Albury	$460,000	$245,000
Taree	$243,500	$189,950
Wagga Wagga	$388,000	$213,750

The other States

With the end of the mining boom in West Australia, housing prices have fallen substantially.

House prices in Perth are currently $605,089 and $382,350 for apartments in local government areas.

In Brisbane the median price for houses is $490,855 with apartments at $371,508.

In Adelaide, the median prices are $479,285 for houses and $292,399 for apartments.

Hints

As rates and taxes on property are calculated in most states on the value of the property, Sydney with its high property values for houses will have the highest annual rates and tax assessment each year.

Stamp duty on the purchase of a home is quite considerable and needs to be taken into account when buying your new home.

First owner's grants

In most states there are first owner's grants available to first home owners, which you as a new migrant need to find out about and take into account when purchasing a new house.

On your arrival, you will need to contact the State Revue Office to ascertain full details of any available concessions and how to use them to your advantage.

In the next chapter, we will look at all the additional costs that need to be taken into account when buying a home, as well as a look at how banks go about granting a mortgage to a new buyer.

10

How to go about buying your first home and pitfalls to avoid

You should think about finance well before you start searching for your home. In Australia, if you sign a contract and then discover that finance is not available, you are still committed to buy the property, unless the contract specifically states that the purchase is *subject to finance.*

If you need a loan or mortgage, and with newcomers this is usually the case, you should find out how much you can borrow before committing yourself to a purchase.

Financial Assistance from the State and Commonwealth

As stated in the previous chapter, as you are buying for the first time in Australia, you may be eligible for financial assistance from the Commonwealth and State Governments. Leaflets about Commonwealth assistance are available from most banks, building societies, estate agents and all Social Security offices.

Financial Assistance from building societies and Banks

Building societies and banks are the most common source of finance for home buyers. Some may prefer you to save with them for a specific period of time before you are considered for a mortgage.

The size of the loan you are given will naturally depend on the family income. Competition for home borrowers is intensive in Australia at present, so shop around, before committing yourself.

Many banks and building societies may include a wife's income when making this assessment, even though she may not be employed on a long term basis.

Depending on the financial institution, rate of interest and the size of your repayments, you can usually borrow up to 80% of the value of the property. The loan will be repayable over a 15 – 25 year period and banks tend to assess the end repayment date according to the borrower's age and the number of years to retirement (65 years of age, in Australia). So, if the borrower is 45 the loan may only be extended for 20 years.

Purchasing through a Real Estate Agency

Most new home buyers will make their purchase through a real estate agent. Therefore, I would recommend that you use several agencies in your search for the perfect home. In this way you will get to see a wide variety of properties and also be able to compare the purchasing deals that are offered to you.

Hints

There are few points to keep in mind when dealing with real estate agencies:

- Remember, buyers are not charged fees by estate agencies; the agency gets a commission from the seller of the property.

- Be quite clear on what you are prepared to spend.

- To avoid wasting your own time, clearly describe the sort of home you are looking for.

Purchasing a Home at auction

It is very common for Australians to sell their homes by auction. Houses to be auctioned will be advertised well in advance giving potential buyers a chance to view the house before the auction.

If you choose to buy a home at auction, you must make sure that you have the necessary bank finance arranged *before you* begin bidding.

Mortgage brokers

You could make life easier for yourself by dealing with a mortgage broker. A mortgage broker will be able to organise your finance rather than going directly to a bank. They deal with all the banks and financial institutions and are likely to get you the maximum mortgage loan from a bank depending on your circumstances.

Mortgage brokers do not charge for their services. They receive their commission from the bank after the settlement of the loan.

Mortgage brokers are usually licenced and regulated by state legislation so you know that you are dealing with a professional.

Hints

Unlike other forms of home purchase in Australia, you are bound by your successful bid, and payment is usually expected 30 to 60 days thereafter.

In some cases, those selling their homes at auction may offer vendor finance at very attractive interest rates. If you take advantage of such finance you will have more time to negotiate with your own bank.

- Be sure that you really want the house you are bidding for. Once you have signed the contract, most states uphold what is called a 'cooling off period' of two to three days. This allows the buyer to cancel the cover note or initial contract if necessary.

- It is not unknown for the auctioneer to have one of his own people bidding in order to push up the price. Take care that you don't get caught up in the excitement of the moment and commit yourself to paying more than you can afford.

Private Sales

Some people sell their homes privately, without the assistance of estate agents. These advertisements are often placed in the classified sections of the major suburban newspapers, as well as in the major daily newspapers. Now more and more houses for sale are offered on the internet.

Purchasing your home

Before you sign any contracts, you must make sure that the house is structurally sound and that it is free of termites. Some home buyers engage an architect, builder or engineer to check the house over before committing themselves to purchase.

Once you have selected a home, your next step will be to *make an offer*. In all the states except New South Wales, once your offer is accepted by the agent/property owner you will have to pay a small holding deposit and sign a *contract note* in good faith. This payment guarantees the sale of the house to you even before you have signed the usual, legally binding contract

New South Wales is the only state which differs in its procedures. In this state the holding deposit and its cover note are *not* regarded as a guarantee of your right to purchase. In fact, the seller may still sell the property to a higher bidder, a process known as *gazumping*.

The sale of a home in New South Wales only becomes legally binding when *there is a contract in writing.*

Once the contract has been signed the buyer usually pays a 10% deposit. If you do not proceed with the purchase you may lose your deposit.

Conveyancing/Final Settlement of Purchase

Final settlement or *conveyancing* of the contract is the last stage of the transaction. The safest way to do this is to employ an experienced solicitor who has been recommended to you by family or friends.

Some people try to save costs by handling their own conveyancing. Do-it-yourself conveyancing kits are readily available from law book shops, on line and from some newsagents, but the procedure is tricky and time-consuming. I would not recommend this to a new immigrant who has no experience of property purchase in Australia.

By law, the seller must provide a statement of matters affecting the property, including details of mortgages, rates, zoning, and so on. In Victoria, this is known as a *Section 32 document*. Your solicitor will carry out all further research on the property to ensure, for example, that the seller really owns the property and has clear title of ownership.

Your solicitor could assist in finalising the mortgage arrangements with the bank or building society.

If all is in order, contracts will be exchanged and you will pay the balance as arranged in 30, 60 or 90 days. You may then move into your home.

Extra Costs

Don't get caught short! Remember as indicated earlier, the price of the house is not your total cost. There are a number of *extras* which you need to include in your financial arrangements. These extra costs will include the following:

- Stamp duty on the purchase price.
- Stamp duty on the mortgage.
- Solicitor's fees, both for conveyancing and the preparation of the mortgage.
- Registration of the mortgage.
- Bank or financial institution charges.
- Titles office registration fees.
- Search and inquiry fees.

This list may add up to many thousands of dollars - so know what is involved before signing the contract.

Insurance

Some financial institutions insist that you insure your property before finalising the loan. Whatever the case, you must include the cost of insuring your new home when calculating the overall sum needed for purchase.

Hints

- The sale of a house usually includes certain fittings already installed such as carpets, air conditioners, light fittings, curtains and blinds. Your estate agent must itemise these in the contract of sale and you should check that they are included. Double checking a few days in advance of the move can prevent unpleasant surprises.

- If you are buying a apartment in a strata title complex (condominium or Sectional Title property) you must know in advance the body corporate fees and the common property areas available to all the tenants.

- Always know your rights and obligations before buying either a house or an apartment.

11

Should you bring your car to Australia or buy one?

Australians are among the most motorised people in the world. Most families own at least one car and many have two. The popularity of the motor car is partly explained by the suburban spread of cities and the distances people travel to work.

Petrol prices are at present around $1.25 to $1.30 cents per litre, but this may change due to world prices for oil.

Buying a Car in Australia

The price of a locally manufactured, small car in Australia, for example, a Toyota or a Ford Laser, would be about $18,000 - $20000 at present, while a family car like a Holden or Falcon would cost about $28,000 - $32,000.

Both Holden and Ford will cease manufacturing in 2017 and you need to consider this in your purchase of a car.

On the exotic side, a top-of-the-range BMW 525e can cost as much as $85,000 plus accessories and government tax while a Mercedes 380 SEL comes in at over $180,000 plus.

Many immigrants, wishing to get extra funds out of their country, decide to bring a car like a Mercedes or BMW with them to Australia for resale. My advice to you if you intend doing this, is to go about it very carefully as there are a number of Australian restrictions which you may know nothing about.

There are a few things you should keep in mind before importing a car to Australia:

- Safety belts have to be installed in both front and rear seats along with other engineering modifications that must comply with Australian safety standards. The modifications will need to qualify under the Registered Workshop Scheme (RAWS) and the required Australian Design Rules (ADR).

- Certain models available overseas are not sold in Australia. This means you will not easily get replacement parts for the vehicle, and this in turn, will influence the price you can ask for it should you sell it.

- Australian Customs regulations require you to keep the car for 12 months. You will have to acquire a bank guarantee in favour of Customs to cover the duty on the car should you find a buyer for it within 12 months.

- Remember that when the vehicle arrives it may be subject to Import Duty of between 5% and 10% of the value of the vehicle plus other small charges like import approval charges, vehicle cleaning and dock transfer which total a further $200 or more. The compliance costs could cost you up to $3000 or more.

- Do your homework thoroughly before you decide on the choice of vehicle to bring out. Go to your local library and get a copy of a major newspaper from the Australian city you will be settling in. Internet sites like *carsales.com* or the Saturday editions often carry the bulk of the week's motor-car advertisements. In this way you can make sure that your car is readily saleable and comparable to others sold in Australia.

Driving Licences

- If you already have a valid driver's licence, be sure to get an international drivers licence before you leave for Australia. This licence will be valid for one year in Australia.

- If you can present your international licence and your original drivers licence, most motor transport departments will only ask you to do the oral test and not the practical test before issuing you with an Australian Licence.

- A driver's licence is always a good thing to have when applying for a job.

- Remember that a driver's licence is also an invaluable form of identification for all transactions in Australia

- All drivers must be insured against injuring other people and damaging other vehicles. This could cost between $400 to $1000 per annum. Check with your local authority as this varies from state to state.

12

The salary structure in Australia

To give you an idea of the salary and wage structure in Australia, the following information has been included based on a survey of salaries in accounting, finance, computing, office support, human resources marketing and IT. The survey was published by Robert Half, one of the largest placement agencies for people in accountancy and related fields. I have selected these areas of employment because at present they are in the greatest demand in Australia.

Abbreviations

S=Sydney, M= Melbourne, B= Brisbane, P = Perth

All figures set out below are in AUD'000

	S	M	B	P
Accountants (newly qualified)	90-127	80-110	80-90	90-12
Management Accountant	70-110	80-100	70-83	80-120
Internal Audit Manager	92-130	110-135	97-115	120-145
Financial Accountant	70-110	80-100	80-105	80-110
Financial Controller	105-150	130-160	115-140	120-160
Payroll Clerk	48-75	50-67	50-58	50-75
Accounts Payable	65-75	70-90	52-60	45-60
Bookkeeper	60-80	65-85	50-65	55-75
Payroll Manager	70-110	85-120	65-88	65-95
Credit Controller	47-60	50-65	48-60	50-55

	S	M	B	P
Commercial Manager	120-150	140-160	95-155	120-170
Receptionist	43-58	43-60	43-55	43-53
Secretary	50-65	50-65	45-60	60-78
HR Administrator	46-55	50-65	50-64	55-67
HR Coordinator	55-70	55-65	62-75	60-78
Systems Engineer	75-120	70-110	80-110	80-120
Database Administrator	75-110	70-115	70-115	87-125
IT Manager	120-150	120-155	100-150	95-140
Executive Assistant	65-85	70-90	60-90	60-90
Marketing Assistant	45-60	45-65	45-60	45-63
Word Processing Clerk	42-52	45-60	42-52	43-50
Office Manager	65-80	65-90	60-85	55-80
Audio Typist	48-55	50-55	48-58	45-53
Project Administrator	52-67	55-70	50-70	55-72

The following is the latest weekly earnings by tradesmen according to the Australian Journal for Labour Economics 2015:-

	Weekly Income as an employee	Weekly Income self employed
Electrical, electronic trades	$996	$1010
Mechanical, fabrication trades	$994	$532
Automotive	$957	$575
Construction trades	$956	$717
Production and Transport	$917	$469
Agricultural, horticultural	$777	$686
Labourers	$755	$630
Other trades including Food	$969	$637

13

Finding a job

One of the first tasks facing a new immigrant to Australia is finding a job.

You can begin your preparations for job-hunting before you come to this country by having a *Curriculum Vitae* (C.V.), resume or job history stating your work experience prior to coming to Australia. A well-written C.V. is essential to Australian employers trying to compare your experience with their requirements.

Preparation of a C.V.

It is well worth paying a professional C.V. writer in your home country to prepare a resume for you. If you would prefer to do it yourself, here are a few guidelines to keep in mind:

- State your address, even if it is temporary, and ways of contacting you, such as your email address and phone number
- Your academic qualifications should appear in the introduction.
- Always begin your work history with your *most recent* job and work backwards from there.
- Keep it brief. Do not elaborate too much in the C.V. - it may not be to your advantage to appear to be over qualified for a position. Rather emphasise your skills and versatility.
- Your C.V. need not exceed two or three pages, but should look professionally laid out and easy to read.
- Give the name of one current referee who your prospective employer can contact if desired.

- Make several photocopies of your C.V. and job references as it is a good idea to leave these details with prospective employers or the recruitment agencies.

Sourcing a Job

Most positions in Australia are advertised in newspapers, the internet and trade journals or found through Centrelink.

Newspapers

You should read the employment sections of some major Australian newspapers before you migrate. In this way you will familiarise yourself with the Australian labour market and some of the recruitment agencies that specialise in your field.

The International editions of 'The Australian' (National),'The Age' (Victoria) and the 'Sydney Morning Herald' (New South Wales) may be available for reading in the city library of your home town. These newspapers are also available at the international offices of the Australian Trade Commissioner.

When you arrive, you will find that the majority of positions are advertised in the Saturday editions of these Australian newspapers.

Many websites like "Seek" have become popular and employers are advertising through the internet for staff.

Finance Positions

The Friday edition of the 'Financial Review' carries the bulk of job vacancies for senior financial and management positions in Sydney and New South Wales. This publication is a must if you are in the field of finance.

Trade & Professional Journals

You may also source jobs through Australian trade and professional journals published for your field of work. These might be available in information libraries in your home country.

Centrelink

Migrants who do not have a job should register with Centrelink, which is a free service. You may be eligible to apply for a limited range of government funded job support services through Job Services Australia.

Centrelink offices are located in cities and in all suburbs throughout Australia. Jobs vacant in all areas are posted on their noticeboards and, as their offices are linked by computer, it is immaterial which office you visit. Centrelink also has a professional employment service which handles positions for professionals and graduates.

Recruitment Agencies

Many Australian companies pay professional consultants to recruit staff on their behalf. The job applicant does not pay anything for this service. Some consultants specialise in particular fields of employment.

If you can access current Australian newspapers before you leave your home country, it is worth making a list of the recruitment consultants who specialise in your field. You could then write to them, enclosing your C.V., your employment requirements and the time of your intended arrival in Australia. This will allow consultants to organise interviews for you well in advance.

Ethnic Preference Employment

Local ethnic newspapers, such as the Italian. *Il Globe* in Melbourne, sometimes carry advertisements for jobs that will appeal to members of specific ethnic groups. Similarly with the *Jewish News*.

Industrial Awards

Most trade and related areas of employment in Australia are covered by an Industrial Award. This is an industrially negotiated fixed wage and a salary or wage will be offered to you at these rates.

A call to the local secretary of the Industrial Council or the Union covering your trade will provide you with a guide to the wage or salary you may expect. This source will also give you the normal working conditions for your field of industry, for example minimum hourly rate, number of hours worked per week, annual leave, sick leave, and so on.

The Industrial Award rates do not apply to management staff.

Check also with the Trades Recognition Australia website on www.deewr.gov.au/tra

---

Hints

As a new immigrant you are an 'unknown quantity' to your new employer. For this reason you should not feel put down if you have to accept a position or salary lower than in your home country. As soon as you have proved yourself and acquired an Australian track record, your salary should rise.

You do not have to accept the first position offered to you. Try and make enquiries about the company wishing to employ you through a friend, neighbour or the relevant Union or Industrial Council.

Immigrants to Australia tend to work hard for success in their new country. Employers will not be slow to recognise ability, hard work and creativity.

14

How to buy a franchise business in Australia

Migration to Australia and the opening of franchised retail businesses by migrants and other Australians has been one of the driving factors in the growth of the Australian retail sector.

Many Australians who have left their employment, some with financial equity, and are looking for something new to do, may consider buying a franchise as a way of having a job, and at the same time being their own boss.

Franchising is a good path to follow, as it allows the new retailer, without retail skills, to "piggy back" on an existing successful business model. However, this may not always be so.

Many overseas companies have brought their skills and retail experience from their own home countries to Australia and have opened franchises to expand their network. New migrants will recognise these businesses from their home countries. These include chains like McDonalds, Starbucks and KFC.

Unless you own the property, the fundamental document that allows you to enter into retail business, is the retail lease, which you enter into with the landlord, either directly or through the franchisor. However, the intricacies of negotiating a lease and determining whether you can make a living from a retail business, is no easy task for a newcomer to retail.

If a potential new retailer wants to go into a retail business, these are the options:

- Buying a franchise with one of the many retail franchise businesses currently operating in Australia.
- Finding a shop in a relatively busy shopping centre where the landlord is prepared to accept your lack of retail experience, or in the case of a new migrant, your overseas experience.
- Opening a store in a strip centre or on a free-standing site.

The purchase of a franchise is very much determined by the franchisee's rights and obligations as contained in a number of legal documents.

Remember that before you sign a legal document, you should always read the fine print.

The franchisee needs to know and understand all the implications of the franchising agreement and disclosure statement as well as the lease document. Often it is worth seeking advice if you are uncertain of meanings or implications of what is in these documents. Better safe than sorry where your money and your family's welfare is concerned.

It is worth your while taking the time and the effort to acquaint yourself with the details of your franchise, before you sign the documents. It is always best to be knowledgeable and to be on the winner's side. Remember that knowledge is power and power, will be your strength in your negotiations with a franchisor.

The Advantages and Disadvantages Of Opening a Franchised Retail Business

There are a number of advantages and disadvantages of opening a franchise business:

Advantages:

- You have the right to use an established trade name instead of incurring the cost of establishing your own name or brand.
- There is an immediate entry into the market.
- Your product is more likely to receive public acceptance.
- The franchise is usually a proven business model with a complete franchise format.
- You will receive adequate training from the franchisor and his staff, which will give you a good grounding, especially if you have not been in that area of retail previously.
- Your business will usually form part of a national advertising program that is likely to benefit your sales. As indicated earlier, this comes at a cost, and you may have to pay a contribution such as a percentage of sales, to such a program.
- The franchisor will have established reliable sources of supply and group purchasing through the network and this will result in better bulk discounts for you.
- There is always on-going support if you run into difficulties.
- If you have to sell your business, it could be easier than anticipated as the franchisor may have a pool of potential franchisees wishing to buy an established business.
- The franchisee has already done sufficient research to gauge whether the franchised store will work in a particular location or shopping centre.

Disadvantages:

- As you will be bound to a franchisor for the term of the franchise agreement that can be up to 5 years or more, it is essential that you find a franchisor that is both competent and ethical.
- Not all franchises are soundly based or well run. Speak to a number of other franchisees and canvass their opinions about the franchise and the franchisor.

- You will be bound by the strict format of running a business and unable to buy products outside the established product range.
- As indicated earlier, many franchising systems include charges for display, advertising, administration and IT information, which you may feel is not required. Nevertheless, the costs of these services will continue for the term of the agreement.
- Bad performance by other franchisees in the retail network may adversely affect your business reputation.
- There is no guarantee that the business will work in your particular franchised region or shopping centre.

However, Australia has a very successful franchise retail sector. It is well regulated with good trade practice legislation and an ever improving code of conduct aimed at giving people a fair chance to succeed.

In taking this route to a retail business, a new migrant is likely to be more successful if he takes a franchise in an industry that he knows from his home country. This will ensure that the transition is as easy as possible. It is also advisable to select the sort of franchise where he is most comfortable and confident, and suits his personality.

If you do not have an outward going personality and do not relate easily to new people, it may not be in your best interest to take up a food or restaurant franchise that requires constant interrelationship with customers.

As more and more retailers are franchising their businesses and selling franchisees to new migrants, it is important for a migrant retailer to understand the legal position regarding franchisees in the various states.

The rights of franchisees with regard to their leases have now, in a number of states, been incorporated into retail tenancy legislation. This protects new migrants and others. It is essential then that the franchisee is aware of his rights under the legislation.

In addition, the rights of franchisees and franchisors are now included in a federal Act known as the "Franchising Code of Conduct". All new migrants contemplating going into a franchise must acquaint themselves with the protections given to franchisees under this Code. My book "The Retailers Guide to Lease Negotiation and Administration in Australia" covers the new code in detail

The Franchisees Checklist - Before Proceeding With the Purchase Of a Franchise

The following is an additional checklist that I believe a franchisee should be aware of before entering into the franchise.

The checklist has been divided into a number of sections as follows:

Examining the Retail Product

- Has the product been sold for a number of years in Australia?
- Is the franchise a single product franchise and sold throughout the year. For instance, if it is an ice cream franchise, what will you sell in the winter months?
- Is the product likely to be replaced by new technology in the short or medium term? How well placed is the franchisor to cope with such change if it should occur?
- Is the product capable of being sold on the internet?
- Does the company use the internet, face book or twitter as a marketing tool?
- Has the product particular qualities that give it a distinct advantage over its competitors?
- Is the product in a growth section of the retail market?
- Is the product exploiting a fad or current fashion which may be short lived?
- How competitive is the market for the product?
- How competitive is the price of the product?

- Will competitiveness be maintained?
- Is there the possibility of over saturation in the market for that product?
- What is the source of supply of the product? Is it a local or imported? If imported it may be subject to currency fluctuations?
- Are future supplies of the product certain?
- Are there alternative sources of supply of the product if a main supplier goes out of business?
- Are the products based on a trade mark or patent? If so, how long, have these trademarks or patents to run?
- Has the franchisor got a long term contract with the supplier for the products?
- Are the products supported by guarantees and service facility support?
- Can a manufacturer easily by-pass a franchisor and set up his own supply to the market?
- What is the reputation of the product as to reliability in the minds of the public?
- What is the reputation of the main supplier?
- If it is a food product, has it undergone certification from the appropriate government authority?
- Do discount stores and mini major stores also sell the product and cut prices? If so, you could go out of business. This occurred recently in the photo processing industry.
- Are volume discounts earned from group purchases from one supplier passed on to all franchisees?

Checking the Franchisor's financial position and business ability

- Always take out a credit check on the franchisor, either through your bank or a credit agency. Remember the financial failure of a franchisor may result in you, the franchisee loosing your entire investment

- How long has the franchisor been in business?
- Has the franchisor previously been in total control of the chain, and thus aware of all the strengths and weaknesses of the business? Is he now selling off the business to raise capital? Or does the franchisor simply have a single store, and is more in the business of selling franchises than running businesses?
- Check the company records of director's interests. Particularly note if the franchisor has no conflicting interest in your main supplier.
- Speak to other franchisees to find out whether the franchisor is approachable and will continue to be, after you sign the agreement and whether you will be happy in being in a long term relationship with the franchisor.
- There should be a manual which clearly sets out all you need to know about the business and the product?

Bear in mind that there are a number of legal and other considerations to take into account, when purchasing a franchise. Therefore, it is best to find out as much as possible about these by reading available information and seeking legal advice.

The Decision To Go Into Franchising

Approach your decision with a cool head. Do not be impulsive or influenced by friends or family as your savings and possibly your future is at steak.

Once you have decided to buy a franchise, if you follow the rules and decisions laid out by the franchisor you should be successful.

15

Converting overseas qualifications to work in Australia

Tradespeople & Artisans

If you were qualified to practice a trade in your home country, for example, a boilermaker, toolmaker, sheet metal worker, electrician or engineer, you can contact your local union office who will guide you on how to convert an overseas qualification to a local one.

A useful website for a new migrant is the Australian Skills Recognition on www.immi.gov.au/asri.

If you started working towards a qualification in any of the following trades before leaving your home country, you may be able to complete your training in Australia:

- Agriculture
- Building & Construction Industry
- Food Industry
- Footwear Manufacture
- Furniture Manufacture
- Metal Work
- Vehicle Building

Professional Qualifications

As a new immigrant to Australia with professional qualifications from a university in your home country, you may find that your qualifications are not accepted by the professional bodies in Australia.

It is possible that you will have to return to university or college to study further in certain subjects before your qualification is acceptable in Australia, for example:

- **Pharmacists and doctors** must rewrite entrance examinations in order to practice.
- **Lawyers** are expected to do articles in a legal office before they are accepted.
- **Accountants** - The Australian Society of Accountants recognises certain accounting societies and bodies in other countries. Your membership with one of these bodies is accepted as proof of your qualification and experience, and you may apply for membership of the Society as a provisional member or associate.

Hints

My advice to a new immigrant who has a professional qualification as follows: before you leave your home country, write to the body representing your profession in Australia and enquire about converting your qualification.

You can write to: The Committee on Overseas Professional Qualifications.

If you are from a British Commonwealth country, or a country where the professional qualification is based on the British code, you may find Australian acceptance easier.

16

The status of women

Working Women

Australia is a non-discriminatory society with the rights of women entrenched by an Act of Parliament

The law demands that women and men are treated equally in the workplace. It is illegal to discriminate against women in levels of status or of pay. As a consequence of this recognition, women have risen to positions of authority in business, politics, public service, the arts and the professions.

All Government departments and some companies in the private sector offer all jobs as 'equal opportunity' positions. Selection is on merit irrespective of sex, race or religion.

The law makes it a punishable offence for women to be sexually harassed in the workplace and it is not uncommon to find women in jobs that are traditionally thought of as 'men's territory'. For example, Australian women work as engineers, architects, doctors, machine operators on building sites, tram and taxi drivers and 'jillaroos' (cowgirls on stock farms).

It is not unusual for married women in Australia to retain their maiden names for professional reasons. It is often simpler to do this than to 're-introduce' yourself to established clients (or to introduce yourself to established clients who knew you by your maiden name).

Should a working woman become pregnant, her job is well protected by most industrial agreements. Maternity leave is usually granted for the last weeks before the birth, and for a substantial period after the birth.

Domestic Help

As it is very common in Australia for both partners in a marriage to work, this usually means that the whole family assists with the running of the household. Nonetheless, a working woman who also has small children may still be seen to have 'two jobs', and in such cases many families hire outside domestic help for a few hours a week.

Most Australians do not have full-time live-in help, so new immigrants used to this luxury may find it difficult to adjust. To ease the way, the family could 'practice' housekeeping for some months before leaving for Australia.

Further Study Opportunities for Women

For women who do not work at a job, a good deal of time is taken up with household duties, shopping, and caring for children. Provided that suitable childcare is available, or children are at school, it is often stimulating to have outside interests, hobbies and educational opportunities.

With this in mind, a number of organisations arrange courses which run for a few hours during the day or in the evening. The courses cover a wide range of stimulating and inventive topics such as languages, creative writing, poetry, art, computer skills, exercise, yoga, meditation. Many of these courses may be free. Contact your local community council office for further information.

For the new immigrant mother who is isolated at home, or is not meeting people in the workplace, these courses also provide a venue for meeting new people and sharing interests and ideas.

Skills developed in these courses could be of value later if a woman chooses to enter the job market. In fact, many Australian women return to formal study so as to improve their present work status or if it helps them to prepare for a completely new career.

Study and Career Guidance

Career advisors are employed by Career Reference Centres throughout Australia to give free guidance and advice to people wanting to study.

Universities, technical colleges and colleges of further education also provide career guidance counselling free of charge.

Marital Difficulties and crisis situations

If a woman experiences difficulties in her marriage, she may contact a marriage guidance counsellor or social worker at the Family Courts which function throughout Australia. This service is completely free of charge.

Women who do not speak English and need marriage counselling or legal assistance will receive help from experienced interpreters.

The State Governments and some private organisations finance women's refuges (safety homes) where women in crisis situations and their children can find counselling and short term safe accommodation. Lifeline or the Department of Community Development (in the White Pages of the directory) can advise you of the nearest refuge.

If a woman is molested or attacked, or if she fears for her own or her children's safety, she should contact her local police through the emergency numbers listed in the White Pages of the Telephone Book.

17

Until you find a job, are you entitled to unemployment benefits and other support services?

Unemployment benefits

If you are a new immigrant to Australia, you are not entitled to unemployment benefits from Centrelink. You will need to wait 104 weeks before you can access benefits like "Newstart" Allowance or "Youth" Allowance. This is known as the Newly Arrived Residents Waiting Period. Any time in your life spent as an Australian resident can be counted towards the waiting period for benefits.

Note, that there can be exceptions or special circumstances that exempt migrants from the waiting period. Therefore, you should lodge a claim with Centrelink to test whether you are eligible for the exemption

Be certain that you have sufficient funds available to tide you over until you find a job

As part of your permanent residence visa an assurance of support arrangement between an Australian resident or organization might be required, so that you do not rely on Centrelink payments.

Other government assistance

Special benefits

The government provides a payment to new arrivals who are experiencing hardship but are not eligible for a Centrelink payment, called a *special benefit*. The benefit is a crisis payment to help people in severe financial need due to circumstances outside their control.

The circumstances under which this is issued may include a payment to a victim of domestic violence, or a person affected by a natural disaster, such as a fire or flood. Refugees or people who have arrived in Australia on humanitarian visas may be eligible for a special benefit.

Professional assessments

The Assessment Subsidy for Overseas trained professionals (ASDOT) can help overseas trained professionals with the cost of assessments and exams.

Maternity Immunity Allowance

In order to encourage parents to immunise their children the government will pay you a maternity immunisation allowance if your child is fully immunised within the standard vaccination schedule for his or her age. If you are a conscientious objector or there are medical reasons you may get an exemption. This can be claimed on line. However, some schools may refuse admittance if a child is not immunised.

Note: Help is available if necessary through interpreters, by phoning Centrelink anywhere in Australia on 131 202.

18

How long will it take to become an Australian citizen and when will you be entitled to vote?

Citizenship

Citizenship is granted when you have lived in Australia on a valid Australian Visa for four years immediately before applying, which must include the last 12 months as a permanent resident. You must not have been absent from Australia for more than one year in total, in the four year period, including no more than 90 days in the year before applying.

To become a citizen you will also have to satisfy a number of other conditions set out by the Department of Immigration and Citizenship. For example, there must be no doubt of your good character; you must have an adequate knowledge of written and spoken English, and you must understand the responsibilities and privileges attached to Australian Citizenship.

Most people who apply for Australian citizenship are also required to pass a citizenship test. Details of citizenship and application forms are available on www.citizenship.gov.au or by calling 131880.

Before you apply for citizenship get a copy of the citizenship resource book which contains all the information you need to take the citizenship test.

Eligibility for Australian Citizenship

There are several ways in which you may become eligible for Australian citizenship. They are the following:

Naturalisation

You may apply to become a naturalised Australian when you have lived in Australia for 4 years.

By Birth

Anyone born in Australia is automatically an Australian Citizen, irrespective of the parents' nationality.

By Descent

If one of your parents is an Australian Citizen but you were born overseas, you are automatically eligible for Citizenship.

To qualify for citizenship by descent, births should be registered at an Australian Consulate within five years.

Voting in Australia

Australia has four main political parties: The Australian Labour Party, The Liberal Party, The National Party and The Greens Party.

It is usual for the National and Liberal Parties to form a coalition if they are elected to the Federal Government.

The current statutory life of a parliament is three years. However, it is not at all unusual for Australians to go to the polls more frequently than this. Governments have the right to call early elections if necessary - and they often do.

> **Note**
>
> Once you have become a naturalised citizen you are under legal obligation to register as a voter with the Electoral Commission in your area. You will find the address of the nearest Electoral Commission office in the front of the White Pages telephone directory. It is compulsory to vote in all federal and state elections.

Ratepayers' voting obligations

Even if you are not yet a Citizen, the moment you become a ratepayer you will be expected to vote in the Council Elections of your Municipality (Municipal Elections).

> **Note**
>
> It is *compulsory* to vote in Municipal Elections and failure to do so results in an automatic fine.
>
> You will be voting for councillors who will in turn elect one of their number as Mayor of your Municipality.
>
> Municipal elections are sometimes contested on Party lines, but just as often the candidates will be independents.
>
> Even if you are not yet eligible to vote in local or Federal elections, you are entitled to appeal to your local Member of Parliament if you have any problems relating to your constituency.
>
> This is in fact welcomed by Members of Parliament as it assists them to keep in touch with the needs and problems of their Electorate.

19

If your child is born in Australia, how do you register the birth?

If you are pregnant when you decide to emigrate to Australia or have come to Australia on a" look see" and are likely to give birth whilst you are in Australia, there are some rulings that will apply to the birth:

- Every child born in Australia must be registered with the Registrar of Births, Deaths and Marriages.
- Registration must be carried out within 60 days of the birth, even if the child is stillborn.
- The Act requires both parents to complete and sign the registration form.
- Naming your child is a matter of choice. For your child's family name you can use the mother's name, the father's name or a combination of the two with or without a hyphen.
- You may not choose a name that is obscene, offensive, unreasonably long or contrary to the public interest.
- If your child is born out of wedlock, you may choose to register it in your own or in the father's name. The father must, of course, agree to the child taking his name.
- If you do not provide the father's details, the child will automatically take your surname.

Birth Certificates

A birth certificate is a very important document in Australia. It is essential in matters far beyond merely establishing your age.

Here are some of the occasions when you will be asked to produce your Birth Certificate.

- When you marry, you will have to show your birth certificate to the court official or minister of religion.
- If you apply for a passport, the passport office will require your Birth Certificate.
- To claim Social Security benefits, you may be asked to produce your Birth Certificate as proof of your identity.

20

Is there military service in Australia?

No new immigrant is required to serve in the armed forces in Australia. Compulsory conscription was abandoned in Australia in 1972 during the Whitlam Government's period of office.

The Australian Permanent and Reserve Forces now operate on a completely voluntary basis. Nevertheless, the Government encourages able-bodied men and women to join the Army, Air force or Navy Reserves, and makes ample provision for people who wish to undergo military training, or to remain on call for the Army Reserves. Some people may use the Air force or Army to enhance a career in engineering, administration, medicine, logistics, hospitality, or to pursue a trade.

If you are an employee of the Public Service, you are entitled by law to take time off to serve in the Reserves. Likewise, most private companies will give reservists time off, apart from annual leave, to serve up to 30 days per annum.

If for example, you are a Reservist in the Air Force, you are paid tax free for each day attended. Add to that a service allowance, free food, uniforms and accommodation.

21

How does the Australian taxation system operate?

The Australian Income Tax system has undergone some radical changes in the last few years. The following information simplifies the system.

Unless you are an accountant or lawyer familiar with the Income Tax Act, I would advise a new immigrant to use an Income Tax Agent for any taxation advice.

Income Tax Agents

In Australia, there are several companies such as H & R Block & Co, and others that specialise as tax agents. These agencies operate from street-level offices in most suburbs. Their main services are in tax advice and in preparing tax returns for clients.

Most accounting firms also act as Tax Agents, so the accountant who handle your business and personal financial affairs should be able to advise you fully on the tax laws and requirements in this country.

Though you are now eligible to lodge your tax return online with e-tax, I would not recommend this in the first year or two of your arrival in Australia. Use a tax agent instead in these early years.

The Basic Tax Structure

Income Tax is levied only by the Commonwealth of Australia and not the individual states.

The State Governments raise revenue by way of stamp duties on land transactions, mortgages and similar regional based taxes.

To give a new immigrant a broad idea of the tax structure in Australia, the following is a summary of its major features:

PAYE - Pay As You Earn

If you are a wage earner your employer will deduct PAYE from your weekly or monthly wages.

PAYE deductions are paid by your employer to the tax office monthly.

At the end of the tax year, which is 30th June, each employee receives a Group Certificate. This shows your total earnings, as well as deductions for tax, superannuation contributions, union levies, and so on. It is essential to have the certificate when you fill in your Tax Return forms.

Before you start work you should apply to your nearest Tax Office for a tax file number (TFN). The TFN is a unique number issued to individuals and organizations for identification and record keeping purposes. It is important to keep your TFN secure. Allowing someone else to use your TFN can cause you serious problems.

If you are thinking of running a business in Australia, you will need a TFN and an Australian business number (ABN). You will also have to register for Goods and Services Tax (GST). Australian law requires you to pay money into a superannuation account for each person you employ.

From the 2015/16 year-end, you will not be required to lodge a tax return if you taxable income will be below the tax free threshold of $18,200.

To help business and individuals understand their tax entitlements and obligations, the tax office offers a range of help and assistance products. This includes a free presentation called "Tax in Australia" and it is available as a DVD online. It is available in 15 languages including English. View their website on www.ato.gov.au

Tax on Medicare

Each tax-payer pays an amount to cover Medicare (see Chapter 25). For the 2015/16 year-end, the Medicare levy will be 2% of taxable income, unless you qualify for a reduction or exemption. This levy is added to the tax-payers income tax assessment and collected at the same time as the ordinary tax. If you were not an Australian resident for tax purposes for all of 2015/16 you are exempt from the Medicare levy.

Tax for Married Couples

In Australia, married couples who both work are *taxed separately.* You are individually entitled to the tax-free thresholds and other benefits.

Lodgement of Tax Returns

You have until the 31st of October to lodge your tax return. If you lodge your tax return through an income tax agent you can lodge at a later date.

If you fail to lodge a tax return, unless you are exempt from lodging a return due to the nature of your income, or because of the level of your income, you can be fined to a maximum of $550.

Individual Income Tax Rates

The following tax rates for 2015/2016 apply:

Taxable Income	Tax on this income
$0 - $18200	$Nil
$18,201 - $37,000	19 cents for each dollar over $18200
$37,001 - $80,000	$3,572 plus 32.5 cents for each dollar over $37000
$80,000 - $180,000	$17,547 plus 37 cents for each dollar over $80000
$180,001 and over	$54,547 plus 45 cents for each dollar over $18000

Minors under 18 years of age are taxed differently:-

Taxable Income	Tax on this income
$0 - $416	$Nil
$417-$1,307	65 cents for each dollar over $416
$1,308 and over	45% of total income

Company Tax Rates

If you are contemplating going into business and forming a company, the tax rate is 30 cents in the dollar. This is comparable with the top individual tax rate of 45 cents in the dollar. Thus many new migrants thinking of opening a business should discuss with their financial adviser the concept of trading as a company or even a family trust

Provisional Tax-payers

If you are self-employed or if you free-lance in addition to your full-time employment, or earn interest or dividends from investments, you might be classified as a Provisional Taxpayer.

The tricky part of being a provisional tax-payer is that you have to pay tax in advance. For a new immigrant starting your own business, it could be a rather heavy tax burden when, after 18 months, you find that you are assessed not only for the previous year, but also have to pay provisional tax for the following year! Therefore, putting some money aside to pay for your provisional tax maybe helpful.

Tax on Foreign Investments

If you are an Australian Resident you will be required to pay tax on your income from all sources. This includes salary, rents, royalties, dividends and interests paid to you *in* or *out* of Australia.

You will then be given a credit on any income for taxation purposes, based upon the amount of tax you have actually paid in the foreign country.

Capital Gains Tax

From 19th September, 1985, all capital profits on the sale of assets acquired after that date became taxable. The only exception to this ruling applies to the sale of the family home. For assets acquired prior to that date there is no GST payable.

The tax is subject to an inflation growth factor allowance to the 'Base cost' of the asset each year till date of sale.

In 1999, indexation on capital gains ceased. Subsequent gains on assets held for more than one year are reduced by 50% for individuals and 33% for superannuation funds. Capital gains by companies are not discounted.

Tax on Dividends

Dividends received from companies that have paid the full rate of tax on their profits will be free of tax. This is known 'fully franked dividends'.

If the full tax is not paid by the company the tax-free amount will be apportioned accordingly.

Fringe Benefits Tax

Australia has a Fringe Benefits Tax. If an employer gives the employee, as part of his salary, 'perks' such as a company car, interest free loans or free housing, these fringe benefits are assessed and the *employer* is taxed on their value, not the employee.

Understandably, employers are now less keen to offer these benefits as part of the salary package.

GST

Australia operates a goods and services tax (GST), which is payable on all purchases and must be charged on all sales. If you are in business, you can offset the GST charged on sales against the GST paid on purchases.

If you as a new migrant are contemplating going into business, you will need to register for GST if your annual turnover exceeds A$75000

Of course, there are many other provisions of the Income Tax Act, too detailed to be discussed here, which apply to personal and business taxation. A look at the Tax office website as indicated previously will be most beneficial.

Superannuation

Your employer is obliged by law, as part of the employee's entitlement, to contribute on his or her behalf to an industry or nominated superannuation fund. At present the amount of entitlement is 9% You are entitled to this when you retire.

22

How to open a bank account

Australia has a sophisticated banking and monetary system catering for all customer needs.

There is also great competition to attract retail customers. If you are bringing funds with you, you will be welcomed by most banks and building societies as a new customer. Thus, you should take time to shop around for a bank which offers services most suited to your needs.

Numerous Australian banks offer a full retail banking service, and the largest of these are:

- ANZ Bank
- Commonwealth Bank
- National Australia Bank
- Westpac Banking Corporation
- Foreign Banks

A number of large overseas banks are also trading in Australia. These include Citibank, HSBC, Rabo Bank, ING. As an immigrant, some of these banks may be familiar to you in your home country:

Building Societies

As well as offering the usual investment services and home loans, the building societies compete very closely with retail banks and each other.

Most Building Societies provide for ordinary banking requirements of the man in the street by offering their clients savings accounts at excellent interest rates, cheque and automatic teller facilities. Many building societies have recently become banks.

Making Your Introduction

As a new immigrant, you will probably find that your first contact with the bank occurs when you deposit your initial bank draft. This draft will have been issued by your home bank in favour of an Australian bank and will stand as a form of introduction for you.

You should use this opportunity to open a cheque account at the same branch as you will have already established some credit-worthiness through depositing the bank draft.

While opening a cheque account, you could ask the bank to open an investment account for you. This establishes a history of investment with the bank and will stand you in good stead if you want to borrow for a home mortgage.

Also apply for your automatic teller card. This will allow you to draw cash at any automatic teller or branch of your bank.

If you have a credit card like a Visa or MasterCard you may wish to convert it to a card issued by the bank. This will at the same time allow you to establish a new line of credit with your bank which will help you cope with the costs of settling in.

Hints

- If you are arriving in Australia with a confirmed job offer, you will find that banks often extend themselves for staff of their clients. Banking with the same institution as your employer can give you added creditability if you require a loan or mortgage in the future.

- Most banks employ advisors who speak several languages and can assist immigrants in their own language.

- Some of the large banks have geared themselves especially to assist migrants. They offer advice on employment, education, housing, social services, overseas money transfers, migration of relatives and friends.

23

The child care system in Australia

Many new immigrants arriving in Australia with their families find that both husbands and wives have to work. As this is very common here, Australia is well geared towards caring for children below school age.

These are some of the child care choices for children less than five years of age in Victoria, but many states have a similar structure:

- Private child care centres.
- Community child care centres (not for profit centres).
- Family day care-up to four, where pre-school children are cared for in the carer's home.
- In addition to childcare some centres offer playgroups for parents who want to stay with their child while they socialise with other children.
- Private and Community Centre Based Care (also known as Long Day Care)

They are usually run by private companies, local councils, community organisations, individuals, non- profit organisations or by employers for their staff.

Child care is run by qualified staff and usually open Monday to Friday from 7.30 am to 6 pm. Children are usually grouped according to age and their development stage.

All centres must be licenced and carefully regulated with strict rules as to the running and maintenance of the centres, the quality of care, food provided and the number of children in attendance.

Waiting Lists are common due to the high demand so register as early as you can after arriving in Australia.

Most long day care centres will have an early education component in their program, so children will learn as they are cared for.

The cost of such centres range from $80 to $120 dollars per day or more. However if the centres are approved child care services, the family using the service may be eligible for Child Care Benefit and Child Care Rebate as approved by Centrelink.

Family day care

With family care, carers look after children aged from 6 weeks to 6 years who are not yet in school, in their own home. In certain circumstances they may also provide care for older school aged children. All carers must be trained in first aid and have undergone the Working with Children Check. From 2014 all carers needed to have a certificate III level early childhood education and care qualification

The hours of care are flexible. Carers can provide care for the whole day or part of the day. Some carers offer overnight or weekend assistance. This may suit new migrants who are on call or work shifts.

The cost of such family day care ranges from $6.00 to $10.00 per hour approximately. Again you may be able to access Child Care Benefits and the Child Care Rebate to offset these costs

Home care

Home care is similar to family day care except that the professional carer looks after the child in the child's home. However, this is not widely available. It is mostly used where other forms of care are not suitable.

This will be the case where the child lives with another child, who has an illness or disability or where the parents have a disability which does not allow them to look after the child.

This service may require a nanny or au pair, is usually supplied by specialist agencies found in the yellow pages. It is important that you check the references of the nanny or au pair provided.

The cost of nannies:

- If they live in your home, the cost ranges from $15 to $30 per hour.
- The cost ranges from $20 to $40 per hour when they live outside your home.
- An au pair living in your home will cost $88 to $125 per week.

Other care services include outside school hours care, where the centres are located on primary school sites in the school hall or playground. Many centres offer a snack and exercise program. Again childcare rebates are available for this program.

Most local governments keep a list of the childcare options available in the local area so check their websites. They will also have a list of playgroups where carers can bring children to socialise with other children, and to learn social skills. These groups are usually free but may incur a small fee of $5 per session.

Government assistance for child care

Child Care Benefit

- The Child Care Benefit reduces the cost of your total child care fees.
- It is available to you if you are a parent, foster parent or grandparent with a child in your care who is attending child care approved for the purposes of the Child Care Benefit or registered with the Government.

- Approved child care for the purposes of obtaining the benefit include; long day care, family day care, outside school hours care, vacation care, in-home care, and occasional care.

Child Care Rebate

- The Child Rebate is additional assistance if you use Child Care Benefit approved child care, provided that you are working, studying or training at some time during the week.
- The Child Care Rebate covers 50% of your out of pocket expenses up to an annual cap which for 2015/16 was $7500 per child per year.
- Out of pocket expenses are defined as the total child-care fees less the amount of any Child Care Benefit and the Jobs, Education and Training (JET) Child Care Fee assistance that you may be eligible for.
- You have the option to receive your Child Care Rebate paid fortnightly, either to your bank account or through your child care provider as a fee reduction.
- JET Child care assistance provides extra help if you are a parent on an income support payment and looking for work, studying or starting a job. Access to JET is time-limited depending on the study, training or employment activity that an eligible parent undertakes

These benefits are complex. They all require assessment by Centrelink staff. However knowing about them and asking about them during an interview at Centrelink may be to your advantage.

24

Education, schools, colleges and universities in Australia

The Standard Educational Requirements

By law, all Australian children have to attend school regularly from the ages of 5 to 15. These ages may vary slightly in some states and territories. All states and territories require a child to have 13 years of schooling

The school year begins in January and is divided into three or four terms with holidays in-between. The long summer vacation lasts six to eight weeks and school generally starts again towards the end of January. A schedule of school terms is included later in the book.

Most students are encouraged to wear a school uniform. Uniforms and textbooks are not provided free. To cover costs, parents often run school co-operatives to exchange these items or sell them to other parents cheaply.

Pre-school

The school life of an average little Australian begins between the ages of 3 and 5 with attendance at 'kinder' (kindergarten). These preschools may be Government funded or privately administered as indicated earlier.

Pre-school is a gentle start for young children to mix with their peers and to be apart from their family for some time

Primary school

Primary School follows from ages 5 to 12. School is held five days a week from 9am to 3pm for 40 weeks a year. Students learn the primary core subjects of Maths, Science and English. A major part of primary school learning is the skill to live in harmony with other children.

Most children attend a school near to where they live. Children take lunch or snacks to school or can buy food at the canteen

Secondary school

Secondary or High School offers a wide range of subjects to boys and girls aged 12 to 18. In addition to the traditional academic core subjects, all high schools have modern facilities for teaching domestic science, woodwork as well as music, computers and other subjects.

As students progress through high school they are expected to choose a 'stream' of subjects that suit their ability and interests. If they are completing their schooling, at year eleven they make a final choice of subjects to take them through to the end of their school careers.

Students learn about a healthy lifestyle and becoming young adults in a diverse society.

At what age can your child leave school?

Though the age of school leaving varies from state to state, in most states students must complete Year 10.

After Year 10 and until the age of 17 all students have to be:

- In school, or registered for home schooling or
- In approved education or training, for example, TAFE, traineeship, apprenticeship or in full-time, paid employment at an average 25 hours/week or.
- In a combination of work, education and/or training

If your child does not attend school

If your child does not attend school between the age of 6 and 16, you as parents can be prosecuted and fined. If your child has a good reason for not attending school (for example, a medical condition) then you may be able to use it as a defence to prosecution.

Vocational Education

These Vocational Education and Training schools also known as TAFE prepares students for work in many occupations. Students pay a fee to complete a TAFE course. Some employers join a TAFE to train their employees and pay for such training

Universities

Australian universities are of a high standard. They offer three year undergraduate course as well as post graduate studies which take longer to complete.

I would suggest that university students with limited English should enrol in an English program first, which will ensure that their English language skills will enable them to cope with University requirements

Costs for university courses may include "up front" tuition fees. Fees that are paid once the degree is completed are known as the HECS

Incidental fees, books, accommodation and general living costs are also included under the scheme. Graduates can pay back the HECS over a number of years. Students still incur the debt even if they withdraw from university. The HECS laws are currently under review and may change in the next year or so.

The current cost of study in 2016 for selection of courses is as follows:

| Law | $43,566 |
| Medicine | $67,243 |

Vet Science	$73,021
Engineering	$37,212
Accounting	$32,215

A useful website to look at is "Going to University" www.goingtouni. gov.au.

Youth Allowance and Austudy Payments

For young people aged 16-24 the government pays a Youth Allowance. For students twenty-five years and over, the government pays Austudy to provide financial assistance for full time students undertaking approved study. Both payments depend on your income and assets being within certain limits.

However, a 104 week waiting period generally applies to newly arrived residents. Refugees are exempt from this waiting period

Types of schools

Government Schools

Government schools are usually free, and children automatically attend the school closest to their home. Concessional fares on public transport are also granted to all school children.

Meals are not provided at Government schools, but parents may run a school 'tuckshop' selling lunches and snacks to students.

Most Government schools are co-educational and outdoor sporting activities are part of the curriculum for all school children.

Extra School Costs

In addition to school fees there are extra costs that will be incurred during your child's education. These include the cost of books, materials and equipment which can be several hundreds of dollars in year seven and almost double in year twelve. In some government schools additional payments will be required for essential materials including calculators, computers and stationary.

Most schools require that all students wear the same school uniform. Full school uniforms for summer and winter including everything from shoes, hats, physical education material and sports gear can cost you up to $700. Many schools have swap pools or exchange schemes to make such costs cheaper for parents

In addition, parents need to prepare for other student services including after school care, maths coaching or other subjects that require a paid tutor for coaching.

Many schools require students to undertake specific subject excursions for which parents are expected pay. These visits may be to places of cultural or historical importance.

New immigrants who want their children to attend a government school should set aside an initial sum of up to $2,000 per child.

Assistance with educational costs

The education Tax Refund by the federal government was designed as an aid to the cost of education for primary and secondary students. As indicated previously, eligible parents and legal guardians are entitled to receive 50 per cent on some education expenses including computers, educational software, stationary, textbooks and school approved uniforms.

From 2013 this was replaced by the Schoolkids Bonus under which Parents will receive $410 per year for each child in primary school and $820 per child in secondary school. However this bonus is subject to parents' eligibility.

Some states like New South Wales and Queensland offer additional assistance schemes for students living away from home. In Queensland there is also a further textbook and resources allowance for secondary school students.

The Victorian Maintenance Allowance is designed to help low income families. It ranges from $300 per annum for primary school students to $600 per annum for year seven students and $500 per annum for all other secondary school levels. Half of the allowance is paid directly to the school to subsidise the cost of books, excursions and so on. The other half is paid to parents to assist with the cost of uniforms.

Even in government schools the extra costs are quite high. Immigrants, ought to apply to receive the maximum assistance for the education of their children from both the federal and state governments. As stated the amount received will depend on the state in which they live.

All the amounts mentioned are usually subject to cost of living increases and may be higher at the time you migrate.

Private Schools

If you wish, your children can attend a private or an independent school run by a religious denomination or other group. These schools charge tuition fees and cater for boarders as well as day pupils.

The cost of sending your child to a private school is high, but many parents feel that this is worthwhile if their children are to receive a specific cultural or religious education. Many Private Schools are also renowned for their high standards of education, and in some cases parents choose a private school because they feel they provide certain social advantages.

Private School fees rose by as much as 6% to 7% in 2016. If you wish to send your child to a private school, you must understand that the cost may put great pressure on your family and may be beyond the reach and income of many new immigrants.

As an example of the costs you may expect, I have extracted figures from a recently published survey of the annual school fee costs of some of the major private schools in Australia for 2016 for year twelve.

ACT	
Canberra Grammar	$21,040
Canberra Girls Grammar	$20,535
NEW SOUTH WALES	
Presbyterian Ladies College	$30,360
SCEGGS Darlinghurst	$34,327
Scots College	$33,098
Sydney Grammar	$31,419
QUEENSLAND	
Brisbane Grammar School	$24,280
Brisbane Girls Grammar School	$21,700
Anglican Church Grammar School	$21,599
SOUTH AUSTRALIA	
Prince Alfred College	$23,940
Walford	$23,300
VICTORIA	
Geelong Grammar	$35,720
Trinity Grammar	$29,376
Haileybury College	$27,630
WEST AUSTRALIA	
Christ Church Grammar	$25,300

Extra costs

Apart from the cost of school fees, the cost of attending at an Australian private school includes a range of additional costs. These include a once only charge of an application fee and an enrolment fee. Then there are annual charges covering the following costs:

- Building Levies
- Purchase of Computer Equipment like laptops and tablets
- Pre and After School Care
- Additional subject costs like music or sport tuition
- School camps and trips
- Uniforms
- Musical Equipment hire
- School Bus Services
- Book Charges
- Fund Raising Support
- In addition if you child boards at the school you are looking at least at a further $8,000 per annum

In deciding what school to send your children to, you should always look at the table of school performance achieved in matriculation or on the website "Australia the VCE".

If you are sending your child to a government school as indicated earlier you will be able to send your child to the school in the area where you live. The following are the tables of best performing schools in Victoria and New South Wales for 2015 for both government and private schools:

Victoria

- Mount Scopus Memorial College
- Ruyton Girls
- Shellford Girls Gramma
- Mac Robertson Girls High
- Bialik College
- Fintona Girls School

- Melbourne High School
- Ballarat Clarendon College
- Leibler Yavneh College
- Yeshiva College
- Lauriston Girls School
- Presbyterian Ladies College
- Huntingtower School
- Scotch College
- Penleigh & Essendon Grammar
- Trinity Grammar School
- Haileybury Girls College
- Melbourne Girls Grammar
- Strathcona Baptist Girls Grammar
- Nossal High School
- John Momash Science School
- Vicrorian College of Arts School
- Glen Waverley Secondary
- Balwyn High School
- University High
- McKinnon Secondary College
- Melbourne Girls College
- Box Hill High School

NEW SOUTH WALES

- James Ruse Agricultural High
- North Sydney Boys High School
- North SydneyGirls High School
- Baulkham Hills High School
- Sydney Boys High School

- Hornsby Girls High
- Northern Beaches Secondary Schools Manly
- Conservation High School
- Abbotsleigh
- Sydney Grammar
- Reddam House Woollhara
- Fort Street High
- Ascham School
- Girrawheen High School
- Loreto Normanhurst
- Moriah College Bondi Junction
- Emanuel School Randwick
- St George Girls High
- SCEGGS Darlinghurst
- Masada College St Ives
- Normanhurst Boys High
- Loreto Kirribilli
- Hurlstone Agricultural High
- Queenswood School for Girls Mosman
- Pymble Ladies College
- South Australia
- Wilderness School Medindie
- St Peters Collegiate Girls School
- Glenunga International High School
- Stpeters College
- Meridian School
- Pembroke
- Seymour College Glen Osmond
- St Ignatius

- St Dominics Priory,
- Mercedes
- Prince Alfred College Kent
- Heritage CVollege
- St Johns Grammar
- Westminster
- Walford Anglican School

Scholarships

Many Australian schools offer scholarships to children who demonstrate outstanding abilities in a number of nominated areas, ranging from the creative to the performing arts. However students who are most likely to receive scholarships are generally students who demonstrate outstanding academic merits or who are in financial need.

For art and music scholarships, the student may have to sit an examination, attend an interview, be currently enrolled, be practicing a particular faith, play a particular instrument or be from an isolated area.

Academic scholarships are usually awarded on the basis of academic potential. Scholarships may cover the basics like tuition fees as well as materials, textbooks, musical instruments, uniforms and school excursions

If you wish to find more about scholarships you should contact the Australian Council for Educational Research at www.acer.edu.au or speak to the bursar at the school to which you would like to send your children.

The following state websites dealing with scholarships should also be consulted:

NSW

www.det.nsw.edu.au/what-we-offer/awards-scholarships-and-grantsarships

QUEENSLAND

http://education.qld.gov.au/schools/grants

VICTORIA

studentscholarships@edumail.vic.gov.au

25

Family allowances to assist you in supporting and educating your children

In Australia there is *no waiting period* to help new immigrants with family payments to assist with the cost of bringing up their children. Immigrants also have immediate access to health care under Medicare. This will be discussed more fully in the next chapter.

Therefore, as soon as you can, go to the nearest Centrelink office and register for the Family Tax Benefit.

How does the Family Tax Benefit work?

Family Tax Benefits are split into two types of benefits.

Part A

This benefit is paid for each child. The amount is income tested and the amount you receive is based on each family's circumstances. You are eligible if you have a dependent child up to eighteen years of age and you care for the child for at least 35% of the time.

Thus the amount of the benefit depends on your family income, how many children you have and how old they are.

Part B

This benefit gives extra help to single parents with families who have one main income, for example where one parent stays at home to care for a child full-time, or balances some work with a caring for a child. The payment is again income tested.

You may be eligible for the part B benefit if you have a dependent child or student up to the end of the calendar year in which he or she turns eighteen, and you care for the child at least 35% of the time.

The amount of the benefit you receive usually depends on the age of your youngest child. If your circumstances change you must immediately inform Centrelink to ensure that your benefit continues.

From 2016 the benefit supplement is $354.05 per family, but is only paid after the financial year and after you have lodged your tax returns.

Changes include the following:

- If your child stops living with you or your child stops studying.
- If you move house.
- If your child's shared care arrangements change.
- If your partner's income changes.

If you do not tell Centrelink about these changes and you are thus overpaid, you may have to pay the money back. In addition you may be charged with fraud.

Payments will continue to be paid for temporary absences from Australia of up to 13 weeks.

Other Family Benefits

If you share care for a child for at least 14% of the time (two or more nights per fortnight) you may be able to receive Rent Assistance, a Health Care Card, and Remote Area Allowance. Child Care Allowance and access to the lower threshold of the Medicare Safety Net.

There are many other benefits available to new immigrants and you should check with Centrelink, which of these payments may be available for your particular circumstances. Immigrants need to research these benefits carefully as they will prove to be of great value during your settling in period in Australia. The benefits include:

- Youth Allowance
- Single Income Family Supplement
- Rent Assistance
- Parenting Payment
- Parental Leave Pay
- Helping Your Parents
- Education Entry Payment
- Carer Allowance

Note

There are many benefits and allowances given to new immigrants. They are stated in this book and careful reading will give you a very good idea of what is available to help you and your family. A visit to Centrelink will help to clear up any uncertainties you may have. The staff at Centrelink is used to dealing with new immigrants and are usually extremely patient and helpful.

26

How the national health care system (Medicare) works

Medicare

Medicare is the Australian federal health care system and it provides:

- Free or subsidised treatment by health professionals such as doctors, optometrists, dentists and other allied health providers.
- Free treatment and accommodation as a public patient in a public hospital.
- At present, 75% of the Medicare schedule fee for services and procedures if you are a private patient in a public or private hospital (excluding hospital accommodation, theatre fees and medicines).

Australia has a very high standard of advanced medicine and a new immigrant should feel confident of the health services provided.

Bulk billing

Your doctor can choose to bulk bill. This means that the doctor bills Medicare directly for the full payment of the service, and you pay nothing. In addition, you are not charged for any extras like bandages and so on. Alternatively, the doctor will issue you with a payment account and you pay the doctor and claim from Medicare. Both methods boil down to you paying nothing for the consultation.

Seeing a specialist

If you need to see a specialist doctor you can claim from Medicare. However the specialist doctor's fee may be in excess of the Medicare stated amount and you will then be required to pay the excess.

Always ask if the specialst doctor bulk bills or not so you can sort out your financial arrangements accordingly. Some medical practices have the ability to put a Medicare claim directly through to Medicare electronically. Then you will have to only pay the doctor the difference.

Medicare Safety Net Threshold

If you reach a Medicare Safety Net threshold visits to your doctor, or if you are having tests it may end up costing even less. Once a patient's out-of-pocket expenses for medical services reaches the safety net threshold of $447.40 (as at 1 January 2016), all future Medicare services are paid at 100% of the Medicare Benefits Scheduled fee (not at the 85% Medicare rebate), as previously for the remainder of the calendar year for all Medicare cardholders.

Signing up for Medicare

As a new immigrant, you should enrol in Medicare immediately by visiting a Medicare Australia Office which is located in most suburbs and in many shopping centres. You should bring with you your passport, travel documents and permanent visa. Temporary visa holders are not eligible to enrol in Medicare

If all eligibility requirements are met you will be issued with a Medicare number to use until your Medicare card arrives in the mail in about three weeks. The card will have your name and the name of your dependants on it.

In most cases where you have to use medical services, you will have to pay for the medical cost and then later receive the benefit from Medicare. Under current Medicare rules the refund will be paid directly into your bank account.

The Australian Government also helps with the cost of medicines under the Pharmacy Benefits Scheme (PBS). Again if you reach the PBS safety net you will get an additional card from the pharmacist and then you pay a cheaper price for medicines until the end of the year.

Other benefits administered by Medicare

Both Medicare and the PBS are administered by Medicare Australia. Other benefits administered by Medicare Australia include administering the Australian Childhood Immunisation Register, that registers the record details of vaccinations given to a child under seven years of age It also administers The Australian Donor Register and the medical Teen Donor Plan which helps eligible teenagers with the cost of an annual health preventative check. When you visit the Medicare office to register also enquire about the above schemes.

Medicare can also provide you with a kit with a full explanation of Medicare and its services, so again request this from them. It is available in many languages other than English

Private Health Insurance

If you have the means, you may like many Australians, choose to take out private health insurance. Again, many of these providers like BUPA, Medibank Private and others can be found in most suburbs and in shopping centres.

Private health insurance covers some, or all of the costs of treatment to a private patient in private or public hospitals and can extend to some services that Medicare does not cover, such as expensive dental care, optical care and ambulance transport.

The cost of private health insurance can vary. Certain treatment options may be excluded.

If for instance you take out insurance as a young adult, it might exclude certain items like hip replacement.

A family of two in BUPA with a silver level of cover will pay about $375 per month and will have a high level of cover which generally includes a single room in hospital, dental cover, massage, psychological counselling and so on. Fee increases are due from 1 April 2016.

If you take out private health insurance you will be eligible to claim the Private Health Insurance Rebate for tax purposes. Most Australians pay Medicare in the amount they pay in tax. However, in addition, there is a Medicare Levy Surcharge levied on people who earn over $80,000 for singles and $160,000 for couples who do not have private health cover.

The Health Care Card

In certain circumstances, for example if you are a pensioner or a refugee, you will be issued with a Health Care Card. The type of concession or health care card you can claim will depend on:

- The type of income support you receive
- Your Age
- Whether you have dependants

The card entitles you to cheaper health care services and less expensive medicines. Your partner and children may also be covered by the card if it relates to an income support payment. In addition to Medicare Services Concession cards can give you concessions from state and local authorities and from private businesses. Check this concession with your local council as soon as possible as this could reduce some of your council rate charges.

Prescribed Medication

Ask your pharmacist to explain how the cost of prescriptions works. Most essential drugs are on the Government approved medical list. The patient usually pays a nominal fee for these, while the balance is paid by the Government. If you have a health card, you pay a small flat rate for all your prescribed medication. Again check this with your pharmacist as the rate is constantly changing.

27

Will my parents be entitled to draw on an old age pension?

If you are coming to Australia with aged parents or parent's in-law, you may wonder if they qualify for an old-age pension.

The old-age pension is only paid when you have lived in Australia for at least ten years.

To qualify as an Australian resident, you must be living in Australia as:

- An Australian citizen.
- The holder of a permanent residence visa.
- A new Zealand citizen who was assessed before 26 February as "protected".

The only circumstances in which you will be paid a pension without meeting the 10 year residency qualification are unless:

- You are claiming a pension under an international social – security agreement with another country.
- You are a refugee or former refugee.
- You had qualified for a Partner Allowance, Widow Allowance or Widow B pension before your age qualified you for an Age Pension.
- You are a women whose partner died while you were both Australian residents, and you had two years residency immediately before claiming for the Age Pension.

The Old-Age Pension is payable to men of 65 or older and women of 64 and a half years. The amount you receive depends on the results of an income and assets test.

Rates of Pension

The sum you are paid or entitled to depends upon whether you are married or single.

The pension is paid fortnightly and the amount is adjusted in accordance with the rate of inflation on 20 March and 20 September each year.

The current rates of pension payment in Australia are:

- Single $788.40 per fortnight Couples $594.30 each or $1,188.60 combined
- A couple separated due to ill health receives $777.40 each.
- There is a further pension supplement payment in addition to the base pension. The maximum rate of Pension Supplement for singles and each member of a couple separated due to ill health is $64.50 a fortnight and for couples $97.20 a fortnight(combined).

An energy supplement of $14.10 for a single person and each member of a couple separated due to ill health is paid fortnightly and for couples $21.20 per fortnight.

Note

If you are receiving a foreign pension, this may affect the amount of the Age Pension you receive.

Aged parents Visas

An aged parent making a parent visa application will not be eligible to an Aged Pension. The 10 year rule applies to them as well depending on how long your parents will be staying with you. A Contributory Aged Parent

(Temporary) visa subclass 864 is available that is valid for 2 years. You could also apply for the Contributory Aged Parent (resident) allowance. Check this with your Immigration Department in your country of origin or at Centrelink and ascertain if this would be applicable in your case.

Other Allowances for Aged People

Mobility Allowance which helps people who have a disability, illness or injury to participate in approved activities. The allowance helps with transport costs for those who cannot use public transport.

Pharmaceutical Allowance which helps people with the cost of medicines

Telephone Allowance which helps with the cost of maintaining a telephone and home internet service.

The Seniors Card

One of the most important assets an aged person has is the Senior's Card. However there are different eligibility requirements in the various states.

To obtain a seniors card simply pick up an application form from any Australia Post outlet, complete and post it. Allow about 3 weeks for your application form to be processed

Eligibility in Victoria

You must meet each of the following three criteria:

- You must be 60 years of age or over.
- Working less than 35 hours a week in paid employment or fully retired.
- You are a citizen or hold a Permanent Resident Visa.

For any details like renewal or replacement of your senior's card, contact seniorscard@dhhs.vic.gov.au.

All information on a Senior's Card application is subject to privacy.

Eligibility in New South Wales

You must meet all of the three criteria set out below:

- You must be 60 years of age when applying.
- Working no more than 20 hours a week in paid employment.
- You are a citizen or a permanent resident of New South Wales and the holder of a valid Medicare Card.

Eligibility in Queensland

- You must be 65 years of age or over.
- Working less than 35 hours a week in paid employment.
- You are a citizen or hold a permanent resident visa in Queensland and can show that you have lived there for more than 6 months of the year.
- If you are between 60 and 64 working less than 35 hours per week and holder of one of the following cards:
  - ◊ Commonwealth Pensioner Concession Card
  - ◊ Commonwealth Health Care Card
  - ◊ Commonwealth Seniors Health Card
  - ◊ Dept of Veterans Affairs Gold White or Orange card

Eligibility in West Australia

On 1 July 2015 the criteria to apply changed as follows:

- You must be at least 61 years of age or over. This will increase by one year every 2 years to 65 years of age by 2023/4.
- Working less than 25 hours a week in paid employment.
- You are a citizen or hold a permanent resident visa in West Australia.

Eligibility in Tasmania

- A resident of the state.
- 60 years of age or older.
- Not working more than 20 hours per week in paid employment.

Eligibility in South Australia

- A resident of the state.
- 60 years of age or older.
- Not working more than 20 hours per week in paid employment.

While the benefits available to seniors from the use of the Senior's Card are similar in most states, let us look at Victoria, for example, in more detail.

The benefits in Victoria are as follows:

- Discounts from many retailers at over 4000 businesses.
- Tech Savvy seniors program through Telstra.
- Concessions on public transport with a seniors Myki concession card, free travel on metro trains, trams and buses and Vline rail services in two consecutive zones on Saturdays and Sundays, free off-peak travel vouchers each year for travel in Victoria.
- Free entry to Melbourne Museum, Immigration Museum and Scienceworks.
- Exemption from a fishing licence, free seniors magazine and free transport during the Victoria Seniors Festival during October.
- Discounts on electricity with AGL.
- Discounts from leisure centres and sporting good s retailers.
- Discounts on medical and dental care.
- Free vaccinations for seniors particularly for influenza.
- A free booklet of 5 concession stamps and ability to purchase up to 50 concession stamps per year.

- Some rural areas have classes to assist migrant seniors to speak more confidently in social groups. This help is available by contacting seniorsonline.vic.gov.au. In addition, senior migrants are able to apply for a magazine that explains all new forms of assistance to seniors in country areas.

28

Where to live in Australia

Australia is one of the most urbanised countries in the world and the majority of people live in the coastal cities established at the time of early colonisation. Almost half the population of Australia live in Melbourne, Sydney and Perth.

People aspire to having their own home on their own piece of land. Thus, Australian cities are characterised by a large suburban sprawl.

Most immigrants arrive in Australia without roots in the country and their decision of where to live is made according to such things as: a firm job offer, family or cultural connections, the cost of housing, the preferred schooling for their children or the climate. Sometimes the decision is based simply upon the beauty of a particular city.

Sydney and Melbourne have, until recently, been the most popular choices for new immigrants, but lately Perth, Adelaide, Darwin and Brisbane attract new immigrants.

Adelaide

It is sometimes called 'the city of churches' and its character is enriched by parklands and wide boulevards.

Adelaide has a large population of people originating from Germany, and they are largely responsible for the world famous wines produced in the Barossa Valley, close to the city.

The Adelaide Arts Festival, held every two years, attracts some of the world's best performing artists, as well as a huge number of art lovers and tourists.

Brisbane

The tropical climate of Queensland has contributed to the relaxed nature of the beautiful and unusual city of Brisbane.

The city, positioned on the wide curves of the Brisbane River, is charming with its mixture of Victorian buildings and homes built on stilts to allow the cooling air to circulate under them.

Brisbane has undergone substantial modernisation in the last few years and its magnificent coastline tempts many new settlers.

The Gold Coast and Sunshine Coast near Brisbane attract many retirees.

Melbourne

Melbourne is a well-planned city and boasts the greatest number of Victorian buildings in Australia. Tram cars add to the city's links with the past and broad, tree-lined streets, beautiful parks, public gardens and the Yarra River flowing through the city, all contribute to a feeling of graciousness.

The National Gallery and Arts Centre complex is considered to be one of the finest in the world and the new National Tennis Centre is an international first in architecture.

The city is over 60km across and there are many newer suburbs that are being built where migrants tend to live.

Melburnians are sports-mad and have set world records for the number of people attending matches for certain sports.

The coastline is very pretty and the ocean waters are beautifully clear.

Perth

Situated on the west coast of Australia, Perth has in the past tended to suffer from a sense of isolation. Now this lovely, green city has made a concerted effort to attract new immigrants and its thriving harbour has created a cosmopolitan atmosphere. The sunny weather, friendliness and the Swan River dominate the city.

Perth was one of the fastest growing cities in Australia and had more millionaires per head of population than any other city in the country. The declining mining boom has affected the populaton growth in the city.

Sydney

The oldest and largest urban development in Australia, Sydney is renowned as one of the world's most beautiful cities. The inner city overlooks the magnificent Sydney Harbour and famous, multi-sailed Opera House. Inner city suburbs are charming with Victorian and Edwardian-style homes and the beauty of the sea is never far away.

Sydney's fish markets and flea markets are a sight to behold and 'Chinatown' is steeped with the atmosphere of the Orient.

The city is 'fast' and modern and the development of Darling Harbour into the site of exhibition halls, gardens and museums has added immensely to Sydney's atmosphere.

Australian Climatic Conditions in the Capital Cities

Adelaide

- Winter rainfall results in cool, moist winters with contrasting warm, dry summers.
- Maximum winter temperatures of 15°C with a minimum of 7.5°C.
- The weather is greatly influenced by the Mount Lofty Ranges near the city. The mountains can determine rainfall patterns.

- In February, the hottest month, temperatures can soar to 40°C, but average maximum temperatures in summer are 28.5°C during the day and a minimum of 17°C at night.
- Daily sea breezes tend to reduce temperatures in the suburbs along the Gulf of St Vincent.

Brisbane

- A sub-tropical climate with no extreme swings in temperature.
- A Summer maximum temperature of 29°C and a minimum of 21°C.
- The winter maximum is the same as for summer, but the minimum can be 10°C.
- The city often experiences rainstorms and very high humidity in summer; January is the wettest month.
- Brisbane averages about 7.5 hours of sunshine a day.

Melbourne

- Winter rainfall results in fairly cold, wet winters.
- Winter temperatures in July average about 13°C maximum during the day with a night-time minimum of around 6°C.
- Summer north winds occasionally give rise to heatwave conditions and temperatures can soar into the high thirties and low forties Centigrade.
- On average, summer temperatures in January are about 26°C during the day and drop to a pleasant 14°C at night.

Perth

- A short, wet winter from May to August, with most of the annual rainfall occuring in this period.
- Summer maximum temperature of 29°C and a minimum of 21°C.
- Winter maximum 21°C and a minimum of 10°C.

- The 'Fremantle Doctor', a cool sea-breeze, blows in most afternoons and is a key influence on temperatures during the day and night.
- Perth averages about 8 hours of sunshine a day.

Sydney

- Summer rainfall results in Sydney enjoying a generally pleasant climate all year round.
- Summer temperatures average a maximum of 26°C during the day and 18°C at night.
- The city experiences particularly high humidity during the summer months.
- Winters are quite mild with a maximum temperatures of 16°C
- During the day and a night-time minimum of 8°C.

However, lately temperatures in Australia generally have been higher than normal, possibly due to climate change throughout the world.

29

The Australian lifestyle

As a new immigrant you might find the Australian way of life a little puzzling at first. The population of this country comprises of so many different origins that its culture is a melting pot of all who live in it. Added to this, the organisation and mood of the society is quite distinctive - the result of much independent political thinking and planning. The weather, spaciousness and richness of the land also add to the mix of the Australian lifestyle.

Having achieved so much in the short space of 200 years, Australians can be over-sensitive to criticism, of themselves and their country. Most young Australians believe that their country is the best country in the world to live in.

With no immediate threats to their country and their way of life, Australians are usually friendly, cheerful and outgoing. They believe firmly in the principles of democratic equality, personal freedom and independence. Every person is entitled to a 'fair go' - the chance to prove themselves - and there is a decided tendency to sympathise with the underdog.

There is complete religious freedom throughout Australia. All groups have their own centres of worship while most offer social, recreational and benevolent activities to their members.

The standard of living is generally high, with plentiful sunshine and an abundance of inexpensive natural foods. There is great emphasis on a healthy, modern lifestyle and sport can be called a 'national passion'.

Sporting clubs and events are some of the most popular social gathering points for Australian people.

Australian Culture and Leisure-Time

Home life

Family ties are mainly strong in Australia and many people centre their activities as a group in the home. Home entertaining is popular and very informal. In summer many people like to gather outdoors for a 'barbie' (barbecue).

Gardening and home improving are hobbies for many Australians, and the beauty of some suburbs bares testimony to this.

The Media

There is great interest in the media in Australia. Most people are literate and newspapers, magazines and journals are available not only in English but in the languages of most of the major ethnic groups.

Added to this, television is a major source of home entertainment and most capital cities enjoy multi channels. Together with the Cable networks, such as Foxtel and Netflix, there is a broad spectrum of entertainment and international news. Imported programmes on SBS are usually shown in the language of the country of origin with English subtitles.

Radio is well-developed and offers several 'ethnic' stations in the larger cities.

All in all, the Australian media works hard to provide for all ethnic groups in the country as well, and is a real boon to new immigrants trying to keep a link with the 'old country'.

Sport

Most towns and cities are well supplied with public sporting facilities for a wide variety of sports. Organised sports, particularly Rugby League and Rugby Union in Sydney and Brisbane, and Australian Rules football (called 'Footy'), are arranged on both a professional and amateur basis to cater for players and spectators. Soccer, cricket, lawn bowls and tennis are sports with rising numbers of devotees. Snow skiing in winter has become increasingly popular.

In the summer months, Australian families flock to the beaches to swim, surf and sunbathe. (Newcomers with fair skins should be aware that the Australian sunshine is extremely strong and the incidence of skin cancer in this country is one of the highest in the world! Therefore, always wear a hat and sunscreen when outdoors.)

Cultural Life

Australian cultural life thrives with cinemas, theatres, concert halls, discos (nightclubs), social clubs and restaurants.

The state orchestras, ballet, theatre and opera companies are well patronised and often feature world famous performers. The popularity of these arts results in many large, beautiful and specialised venues equipped with the most modern sound and light technology.

There is Governmental support for cultural organisations which encourage Australia's immigrant population to keep traditional art forms alive.

Handcrafts are very popular in Australia and the tapestries, pottery and glassware produced in this country are of world renown

Added to this, film-making, jazz music and modern dance are well represented here and have large followings of devotees.

Shopping in Australia

Shops are usually open 7 days a week from 9 am to 5.30 pm and certain supermarket chains are open 24 hours a day, 7 days a week.

Some cities also allow late-night shopping till 9 pm on one or two nights a week, in particular on Friday nights. This is very convenient for families where both partners work.

Banks and Post Offices are open on Saturday mornings, and Australian shops sell a vast variety of locally manufactured and imported goods that meet most tastes and needs. You will find clothing, furniture and other goods of the most contemporary design.

In Australia, stringent consumer protection laws guard the shopper from poor quality and service.

Most city suburbs and large country towns have at least one modern shopping centre with department stores, supermarkets and small specialist shops.

Families tend to do their weekly shopping at these centres and use neighbourhood general stores for smaller purchases during the week.

Post offices

Post offices are used by many Australians for the payment of accounts such as utilities, and other services.

30

Household pets in Australia

Australians are great pet lovers, but bitter experience has taught the authorities to apply stringent regulations to the importation of pet animals to this country.

In the past, animals were brought to Australia, with little trouble, for domestic and agricultural use, and for the pleasure of the hunt. These imported animals introduced foreign illnesses to the indigenous fauna, which, having no resistance to them, then became victim to epidemics. Some of the new animals also prey upon and deplete the numbers of Australian animals.

The quarantine regulations for animals entering Australia are therefore, stringent and most new immigrants do not bring their pets with them.

Legal Requirements for Owning a Pet

- A dog over six months old must have a licence from the local council, and this must be renewed annually.
- A dog must wear a collar with an identity disc showing the owner's name and address, as well as the registration disc from the council.
- Other household animals, including cats, also require registration with local councils. An identifying disc is desirable.
- Dogs must be kept on a leash in public places and the owner must make sure they do not foul any footpaths.

- You can take out public liability insurance to protect yourself against claims should your dog injure someone or causes any damage.

The RSPCA has a charter for the protection of animals. Cruelty to animals is a criminal offence which can lead to a fine or jail sentence.

Taking your pet with you to Australia

If you wish to bring your pet with you when you migrate, you need to ascertain from the Australian Quarantine Information Service whether your pet will be allowed into Australia. Most dogs, cats and horses are eligible.

Bringing your pet may involve a long air trip and therefore, it is important that you ascertain from your local vet that your pet's health is good enough to survive the journey.

Before you can apply for an import permit your dog or cat has to be micro chipped. The chip must also be compatible and be read by an ISO compatible reader.

Application for an import permit must be submitted with your pet's microchip number to one of the 3 major quarantine stations in Perth, Sydney or Melbourne.

Most permitted animals will have to spend a fairly long period of time in quarantine.

The import of a pet is not an easy process and it may be useful to get an independent company to assist you.

Dogs must be vaccinated against:

- Distemper
- Infectious hepatitis

- Canine parvovirus
- Para-influenza
- Kennel cough

Cats must be vaccinated against:

- Feline enteritis
- Rhinotracheitis
- Calicivirus
- More recently cats are vacinated against Feline HIV virus as well.

31

How to improve your English

Learning English is one of the most important steps you can take as a new migrant towards settling successfully in Australia. If possible try to learn as much English as you can before you arrive in Australia, as it will stand you in good stead.

The Migrant English Program

However, if you do not speak English well this will not be a disadvantage. If you are eligible you can enrol with the Adult Migrant English Program (AMEP) which provides you with free basic English language tuition that will help you deal with everyday social and work situations. My advice is to enrol as soon as possible after your arrival.

This programme provides access to 510 hours of English language tuition to eligible migrants and refugees for a period of 5 years from their visa commencement date, or the number of hours it takes to reach proper functional English, whichever comes first.

Refugees or those migrants who have suffered trauma or torture with very little schooling may be eligible for more hours.

To contact AMEP you should call their special telephone number on 131881 for the price of a local call or go onto their website AMEP which is part of the Department of Immigration and Citizenship

The AMEP offers a number of different ways to learn namely:

- Full Time.
- Part Time.
- Learning at home through distance learning.
- Practicing English with the help of a home tutor.

Free childcare is provided if you have children under school age while you are in a class.

English is not easy to learn and the only way to improve is to keep practicing when you go shopping, visit friends or when you are at home with your family.

How does the learning program work?

You will start by meeting your teacher at one of the centres who will assess your level of English. The teacher will decide whether you should attend full time or part time, and work out a plan to allow you to meet your educational and career plans.

You will then attend regular classes at a learning centre. There are classes during the day, in the evenings and on weekends. If you cannot attend because of job interviews or medical reasons it is customary to phone the teacher and explain why you are not coming.

If you are learning English at home, a teacher will talk to you and help you by phone. You will learn from books and tapes and you will also practise by reading newspapers, filling in forms and writing letters

If you cannot get to a learning centre a tutor may come to your home once a week for one or two hours to help you to learn English through practising speaking, listening, reading and writing.

These are AMEP Learning Centres located in New South Wales, Victoria and West Australia (see appendix attached).

32

Maintaining your cultural and religious links

Since 1945 immigrants have more than doubled the population of Australia, and when seen in this light, it is not surprising that this country is sometimes called a 'land of immigrants'.

With immigrants coming from Europe, Asia, South America and Africa, the population created by this inflow is both a multi-cultural and multi lingual society.

Despite all Australian schools teaching students in the English language, the differing cultural backgrounds of these new immigrants has not been submerged or lost.

Most immigrants work hard to maintain their ethnic ties with 'the old country', and the Government encourages this by subsidising ethnic radio and television stations.

In Melbourne alone there are over 70 weekly newspapers and publications in languages other than English.

Immigrant communities have set up many organisations to help their fellow countrymen when they arrive in Australia, by welcoming them and giving them a sense of belonging to the community.

These ethnic organisations offer counselling to assist in finding employment and accommodation, as well as addressing religious and cultural issues. Many provide social activities and English classes for migrants.

Cultural and religious bodies assisting specific ethnic or religious groups can be found in the Yellow Pages of the telephone directory or on the internet.

33

Rotary and other service clubs in Australia

One of the best methods of integrating into the Australian way of life is through membership of an International Service Club or similar organisation.

Organisations such as Rotary, Lions, Apex, Toastmasters, Rostrum, Toastmistress and similar bodies flourish in Australia. If you are a member of such an organisation in your home city, you will be welcomed here with open arms. Membership will bring you into contact with people who have similar interests to your own.

Membership of Toastmasters made me welcome in any Toastmasters' club in Australia. Even my distinct South African accent was no hindrance and through it I have met a great many interesting people.

I suggest that you visit these service clubs as a guest and you will soon experience the real warmth of Australians to you as a newcomer.

Service Clubs which have international affiliations usually operate the same way in all countries. So provided you know the routine, you should have no problems fitting in.

34

Useful facts about Australian school terms

The school terms are not the same in all states. Therefore, depending on the state in which you are proposing to stay, it is important to know the dates of the school terms. In 2016 the dates are as follows:

New South Wales	
1st Term	29 January to 12 April
2nd Term	29 April to 28 June
3rd Term	15 July to 20 September
4th Term	8 October to 20 December
Queensland	
1st Term	29 January to 28 March
2nd Term	8 April to 21 June
3rd Term	8 July to 20 September
4th Term	7 October to 13 December
South Australia	
1st Term	29 January to 12 April
2nd Term	29 April to 5 July
3rd Term	22 July to 27 September
4th Term	14 October to 13 December

Victoria	
1st Term	29 January to 28 March
2nd Term	15 April to 28 June
3rd Term	15 July to 20 September
4th Term	7 October to 20 December
West Australia	
1st Term	4 February to 19 April
2nd Term	6 May to 5 June
3rd Term	22 July to 27 September
4th Term	14 October to 19 December
ACT	
1st Term	1 February to 12 April
2nd Term	29 April to 5 July
3rd Term	22 July to 27 September
4th Term	14 October to 20 December
Tasmania	
1st Term	4 February to 19 April
2nd Term	6 May to 5 July
3rd Term	22 July to 27 September
4th Term	14 October to 19 December
Northern Territory	
1st Term	25 January to 5 April
2nd Term	15 April to 21 June
3rd Term	22 July to 27 September
4th Term	7 October to 12 December

35

Some useful Australian terminology

Whilst Australians speak English, there are some expressions, and slang terms that are strictly Australian, and which a the migrant should be aware of. Here is a mini dictionary for your convenience.

bathers	swimsuit
bikie	motorcyclist
chook	a chicken
crook (health)	feeling ill
cut lunch	sandwiches
daks	trousers
dill/drongo	idiot
dinkum	real
flake	shark meat
flog	sell
Galah	loudmouth
gooodonyer	term of approval
grog	liquor
hard yakka	hard work
joey	baby kangaroo
knock	criticise
loo	toilet
lollies	sweets/candy
mozzie	mosquito

plate (a plate)	food brought to a party
Pom	Englishman or woman
pot	large mug of beer
ratbag	villain
sheila	a girl
your shout	to pay for a round of drinks
Smoke-o	tea or coffee break
stone	14 pounds in weight
stubby	small beer bottle
supper	after dinner snack
tea	dinner or evening meal
trannie	transistor radio tucker food
ute	pick-up-truck
wowser	killjoy
yobo/yahoo	lout

36

Arrangements and entitlements for New Zealanders in Australia

In 1973 the Trans-Tasman Travel arrangements were introduced in both countries allowing Australian and New Zealand citizens to enter each other's country freely, to visit, live, work and remain indefinitely without the need to apply formally for authority to enter.

From 26 February 2001, the two governments agreed on new bilateral social security arrangements. Under these arrangements, New Zealanders and Australians living in each other's country and reliant on Australian Age Pensions or New Zealand superannuation or Veteran's Pensions were guaranteed continued payments irrespective of which of the two countries they choose to live in.

People who arrive in Australia on a New Zealand passport are generally issued with a Special Category Visa. SCV holders who were in Australia on 26 February 2001 are considered to be protected SCV holders. Those, who arrived after that date are generally considered to be non-protected.

Protected SCV holders qualify as Australian residents and can generally access the full range of Centrelink payments, provided that they are residing in Australia.

New Zealand passport holders who have lived continuously in Australia for 10 years since 26 February 2001, and hold a non-protected SCV, may be able to access a once only payment of the Newstart Allowance,

Sickness Allowance or Youth Allowance. If eligible, payment can be made for a maximum continuous period of up to 6 months.

The Social Security Agreement between Australia and New Zealand may help some New Zealand citizens to be paid Age Pension, Disability Support Pension or Carer Payment. New Zealanders may also be eligible for certain concession cards after a waiting period, and payments from the family assistance office. If you think you qualify check with Centrelink.

The New Zealand Family Relationship visa (subclass461) also enables non-New Zealand citizen family members to accompany Special Category visa holders to Australia, and or allow them to remain onshore lawfully with work rights.

A new agreement entered in 2016 allows New Zealand residents in Australia to be eligible for funding in the same way as Australians, for education at Australian universities and colleges, known as the HECS scheme.

From February 2016, New Zealanders on special category visas who have lived in Australia for five years or more, and who earn above $54,000 are now able to apply for Australian citizenship.

The migration laws affecting New Zealanders are complex and New Zealand Migrants coming to Australia should investigate them in detail before getting onto a plane to come to Australia.

37

The first things to do within 30 days of arriving in Australia

Some people take longer to settle into life in Australia than others. Whilst I have tried to give you the best guide to living in Australia, the following are the most important things you should do as quickly as possible after your arrival

Banking and Finance

- Open a bank account with one of the major banks.
- Request a credit card – either Visa or MasterCard which are most readily accepted in Australian stores.

Drivers Licence

- Apply as soon as possible to exchange you overseas drivers licence for an Australian drivers licence. A driver's licence is the most important form of identity as it contains your photo.

Telephone

- Immediately apply for a telephone or convert your mobile phone to an Australian provider like Telstra or Optus.

Medicare

- Immediately register yourself and your family with Medicare and obtain a Medicare card which you need if you are visiting a doctor.

- Ascertain from your neighbours which doctor's bulk bill in your area. This will save you paying the excess gap costs between the doctor's charges and the Medicare refund.

Benefits from Centrelink

- Register with Centrelink to obtain immediate benefits.
- Visit the Centrelink offices and ascertain from them which of the many benefits and family allowances for new migrants you are eligible for.

Find a school for your children

- Research the schools in the area in which you propose to live. The area in which you live will qualify you for the local school.
- Attendance at school is compulsory, so check with the local school as to the school terms and register your child for school. Children under 12 attend primary school, whilst older children attend high school.

Register for Taxation

- Register with the Taxation office and obtain a tax number.
- If you are going into business it is essential that you find an accountant who can help you with obtaining an ABN number, help you to form a company or family trust to run your business and assist you with registering for GST and fringe business tax.

Find a good lawyer

- From friends and neighbours ascertain the names of a good lawyer who can assist you with the purchase of a house or entering into a lease for an apartment.

Find a good Pharmacy

- If you are on prescription medicines you need to find a good pharmacist who can advise you of the local products that are used here and are equivalent to your overseas prescriptions.

Convert your car to comply with Australian Standards

- If you have brought a car with you from your home country immediately convert your car to local requirements.
- Remember that we drive on the left hand side of the road. Courtesy to other drivers is an Australian way of life so practice this immediately you start driving.
- Buy a street directory from a newsagent or the local automobile office.

Special rights for New Zealanders

- If you are a New Zealander, ascertain what rights and benefits are available to you while you are in Australia.
- Investigate the costs and benefits that would be available to you by joining a private health insurance fund. Medical costs are high in Australia and Medicare does not reimburse all the costs

Become familiar with popular Australia names for products sold in Supermarkets

- Visit your local supermarket and determine the names of products sold in Australia which may be different to those from your home country.

Finding a job

- Whilst unemployment in Australia is presently low at about 5.5% it is essential to find a job as soon as possible.
- Contact Australian employment agencies even before you arrive. Internet sites like "Seek" could also be useful. Newspapers like *The Age*, *The Sydney Morning Herald* and *The Australian* all carry the

majority of advertisements for positions in their Saturday morning editions. Buy these newspapers or research on the internet, in advance of coming or as soon as you arrive.

Connecting Lights water and Gas services

- As soon as you have moved into your residence, connect lights, water and gas. These services are available to most homes in Australia.

- Make sure the previous tenants had their meters read before you move in, so that you do not pay any of their charges.

- Research the market for the best prices. There is much competition between suppliers so insure you get the best deal from the start.

Register to improve your English

- Australia is an English speaking country. Register immediately to learn to speak or improve your English. This will help you considerably when applying for a job.

Translation of your main settlement documents

- Free translation services into English of settlement-related documents, such a birth of marriage certificates, drivers licences, educational and employment documents is available to eligible migrants. Again have this done as soon as possible as this will help with your job applications.

Pick a footy club to support

- As soon as possible pick a football club to support. This will quickly make you feel like an Aussie. Even if you never watch a game in which they play, you will automatically be associated with all the other Australians that support that club.

Appendix

New South Wales AMEP Learning Centre Locations

TAFE NSW Riverina Institute
Albury Campus
Poole Street
Albury NSW 2640
Telephone: 1800 114 707

TAFE NSW New England Institute
Armidale Campus
Block B
Beardy Street
Armidale NSW 2351
Telephone: 1800 114 707

Navitas English Auburn College
3 Mary Street
Auburn NSW 2144
Telephone: 02 9749 3300

TAFE NSW North Coast Institute
Ballina Campus
154–164 Burnett Street
Ballina NSW 2478
Telephone: 1800 114 707

Navitas English Bankstown College
2 Jacobs Street
Bankstown NSW 2200
Telephone: 02 9707 0200

TAFE NSW Western Institute
Bathurst Campus
Panorama Avenue

Bathurst NSW 2795
Telephone: 1800 114 707

TAFE NSW Illawarra Institute
Bega Campus
Barrack Street
Bega NSW 2550
Telephone: 02 4229 0025

Macquarie Community College
Blacktown Campus
Level 2, 125 Main Street
Blacktown NSW 2148
Telephone: 02 9621 4175

TAFE NSW Illawarra Institute
Nowra Campus
60 Beinda Street
Bomaderry NSW 2541
Telephone: 02 4229 0025

City East Community College
98 Bondi Road
Bondi Junction NSW 2022
Telephone: 02 9387 7400

TAFE NSW Western Institute
Broken Hill Campus
248 Argent Street
Broken Hill NSW 2880
Telephone: 1800 114 707

Navitas English Burwood College
3 Railway Parade
Burwood NSW 2134
Telephone: 02 9745 2420

TAFE NSW Northern Sydney Institute
Brookvale Campus
D Block, First Floor
154 Old Pittwater Road
Brookvale NSW 2100
Telephone: 1800 114 707

Navitas English Campbelltown College
Level 3
171–179 Queens Street
Campbelltown NSW 2560
Telephone: 1300 798 111

Navitas English Cabramatta College
Level 1
2 Hughes Street
Cabramatta NSW 2166
Telephone: 02 9912 6500

Navitas English Wynyard College
Level 4
11 York Street
Sydney NSW 2000
Telephone: 02 8246 6822

Navitas English Campsie College
Level 1
59–63 Evaline Street
Campsie NSW 2194
Telephone: 02 9784 2500

TAFE NSW Illawarra Institute
Cooma Campus
66 Commissioner Street
Cooma NSW 2630
Telephone: 02 4229 0025

TAFE NSW North Coast Institute
Coffs Harbour Campus
Glenreagh Street
Coffs Harbour NSW 2450
Telephone: 1800 114 707

TAFE NSW Western Institute
Dubbo Campus
Myall Street
Dubbo NSW 2830
Telephone: 1800 114 707

TAFE NSW Riverina Institute
Deniliquin Campus
Corner Poitiers and Macauley Streets
Deniliquin NSW 2710
Telephone: 1800 114 707

Navitas English Fairfield College
6–8 Alan Street
Fairfield NSW 2166
Telephone: 02 9912 6600

Macquarie Community College
Ermington Campus
Suite 6B/10
Betty Cuthbert Avenue
Ermington NSW 2115
Telephone: 02 9684 5111

TAFE NSW Hunter Institute
Glendale Campus
Frederick Street
Glendale NSW 2285
Telephone: 02 4930 2954

TAFE NSW Western Institute
Forbes Campus
Corner Browne and Harold Street
Forbes NSW 2871
Telephone: 1800 114 707

TAFE NSW Hunter Institute
Gosford Campus
Henry Parry Drive and Margin Street
Gosford NSW 2250
Telephone: 02 4930 2954

TAFE NSW New England Institute
Glen Innes Campus
Grey Street
Glen Innes NSW 2370
Telephone: 1800 114 707

TAFE NSW North Coast Institute
Grafton Campus
Craig Street
Grafton NSW 2460
Telephone: 1800 114 707

TAFE NSW Illawarra Institute
Goulburn Campus
Corner Verner and View Street
Goulburn NSW 2580
Telephone: 02 4229 0025

TAFE NSW Northern Sydney Institute
Hornsby Campus
205 Pacific Highway
Hornsby NSW 2077
Telephone: 1800 114 70

TAFE NSW Riverina Institute
Griffith Campus
Neville Place
Griffith NSW 2680
Telephone: 1800 114 707

TAFE NSW New England Institute
Inverell Campus
Corner Wood and Evans Street
Inverell NSW 2360
Telephone: 1800 114 707

Navitas English Hurstville College
Level 2
7–11 The Avenue
Hurstville NSW 2220
Telephone: 02 9598 3800

TAFE NSW North Coast Institute
Kingscliff Campus
Cudgen Road
Kingscliff NSW 2487
Telephone: 1800 114 707

TAFE NSW Riverina Institute
Leeton Campus
Palm Avenue
Leeton NSW 2705
Telephone: 1800 114 707

TAFE NSW North Coast Institute
Lismore Campus
Conway Street
Lismore NSW 2480
Telephone: 1800 114 707

TAFE NSW Western Institute
Lithgow Campus
Block A
Hill Street
Lithgow NSW 2790
Telephone: 1800 114 707

Navitas English Liverpool College
24 Scott Street
Liverpool NSW 2170
Telephone: 02 8738 0300

TAFE NSW Northern Sydney Institute
Meadowbank Campus
See Street
Meadowbank NSW 2114
Telephone: 1800 114 707

TAFE NSW North Coast Institute
Macksville Campus
5–9 West Street
Macksville NSW 2447
Telephone: 1800 114 707

TAFE NSW North Coast Institute
MacLean Campus
Wombah Street
MacLean NSW 2484
Telephone: 1800 114 707

TAFE NSW Hunter Institute
Maitland Campus
Corner Ferraby Drive and New England Highway
Metford NSW 2323
Telephone: 02 4930 2954

TAFE NSW Illawarra Institute
Moruya Campus
2857 Princes Highway
Moruya NSW 2537
Telephone: 02 4229 0025

TAFE NSW Illawarra Institute
Moss Vale Campus
Kirkham Street
Moss Vale NSW 2577
Telephone: 02 4229 0025

Macquarie Community College
Mount Druitt Campus
55 Hythe Street
Mount Druitt NSW 2770
Telephone: 1800 114 707

TAFE NSW Western Institute
Mudgee Campus
2 Short Street

Mudgee NSW 2850
Telephone: 1800 114 707

TAFE NSW North Coast Institute
Murwillumbah Campus
Murwillumbah Street
Murwillumbah NSW 2484
Telephone: 1800 114 707

TAFE NSW New England Institute
Narrabri Campus
87 Barwan Street
Narrabri NSW 2390
Telephone: 1800 114 707

TAFE NSW Riverina Institute
Narrandera Campus
54–68 Elwin Street
Narrandera NSW 2700
Telephone: 1800 114 707

TAFE NSW Illawarra institute
Shellharbour Campus
11 College Avenue
Oaks Flats NSW 2529
Telephone: 02 4229 0025

TAFE NSW Western Institute
Orange Campus
March Street
Orange NSW 2800
Telephone: 1800 114 707

TAFE NSW Western Institute
Parkes Campus
25 Bushman Street
Parkes NSW 2870
Telephone: 1800 114 707

Navitas English Parramatta College
1/7 Hassall Street
Parramatta NSW 2150
Telephone: 02 9685 7100

TAFE NSW North Coast Institute
Port Macquarie Campus
Widderson Street
Port Macquarie NSW 2444
Telephone: 1800 114 707

TAFE NSW Illawarra Institute
Queanbeyan Campus
Corner Buttle and MacQuoid Streets
Queanbeyan NSW 2620
Telephone: 02 4229 0025

TAFE NSW Hunter Institute
Singleton Campus
York Street
Singleton NSW 2297
Telephone: 02 4930 2954

TAFE NSW Northern Sydney Institute
St Leonards Campus
Building P
213 Pacific Highway
St Leonards NSW 2065
Telephone: 1800 114 707

TAFE NSW New England Institute
Tamworth Campus
Janison Street
Tamworth NSW 2340
Telephone: 1800 114 707

TAFE NSW North Coast Institute
Taree Campus
Montgomery Crescent
Taree NSW 2340
Telephone: 1800 114 707

TAFE NSW Hunter Institute
Newcastle Campus
Maitland Road
Tighes Hill NSW 2297
Telephone: 02 4930 2954

TAFE NSW Riverina Institute
Tumut Campus
Corner Capper and Howick Streets
Tumut NSW 2720
Telephone: 1800 114 707

TAFE NSW North Coast Institute
Great Lakes Campus
The Northern Parkway
Tuncurry NSW 2428
Telephone: 1800 114 707

TAFE NSW Riverina Institute
Wagga Wagga Campus
Corner Coleman and Macleay Street
Wagga Wagga NSW 2650
Telephone: 1800 114 707

TAFE NSW Illawarra Institute
Wollongong Campus
Foleys Road
Wollongong NSW 2500
Telephone: 02 4229 0025

TAFE NSW Illawarra Institute
West Wollongong Campus
36 Gladstone Avenue
Wollongong NSW 2500
Telephone: 02 4229 0025

TAFE NSW Riverina Institute
Young Campus
Caple Street
Young NSW 2194
Telephone: 1800 114 707

Victoria AMEP Learning Centre Locations

Wingate Avenue Community Centre
Building 13 A
Wingate Avenue
Ascot Vale VIC 3032
Telephone: 03 9376 5244

Community College East Gippsland
Dalmahoy Street
Bairnsdale VIC 3875
Telephone: 03 5152 2899

Ballarat University SMB Campus
Ballarat Campus
Lydiard Street South
Ballarat VIC 3353
Telephone: 03 5327 8091

Bendigo Regional Institute of TAFE
Bendigo Campus
136 Mc Crae Street Campus
Bendigo VIC 3552
Telephone: 03 5434 1439

Outer Eastern Literacy Program Incorporated
C/– Boronia Library
Park Crescent
Boronia VIC 3155
Telephone: 03 9762 4211

AMES Box Hill
34-36 Prospect Street
Box Hill VIC 3128

NMIT Broadmeadows
Corner of Belfast and Blair Streets
Broadmeadows VIC 3047
Telephone: 03 9309 2833

Kangan Institute
Pearcedale Parade
Broadmeadows VIC 3047
Telephone: 03 9279 2446

Carlton Neighbourhood Learning Centre
Incorporated
20 Princes Street
Carlton VIC 3054
Telephone: 03 9347 7072

Royal Melbourne Institute of Technology (RMIT)
Level 2, Building 514
25 Dawson Street
Brunswick VIC 3057
Telephone:
03 9925 9481
03 9925 9494

Holmesglen Institute of TAFE
Chadstone Campus
Batesford Road
Chadstone VIC 3148
Telephone: 03 9564 1977

Bendigo TAFE (BRIT)
Castlemaine Campus
65 Templeton Street
Castlemaine VIC 3450
Telephone: 03 5471 1907

Corangamite District Adult Education Group
124 Manifold Street
Camperdown VIC 3260
Telephone: 03 5593 2920

Waverly Adult Literacy Program
34 Amaroo Street
Chadstone VIC 3148
Telephone: 03 9807 2322

Goulburn Ovens Institute of TAFE (GO TAFE)
43-45 Punt Road
Cobram VIC 3644
Telephone: 03 5833 2578

Cheltenham Community Centre
8 Chesterville Road
Cheltenham VIC 3192
Telephone: 03 9583 0851

Otway Community College
6 Murray Street
Colac VIC 3250
Telephone: 03 5231 9500

Moreland Adult Education
13 Munro Street
Coburg VIC 3058
Telephone: 03 9383 7943

Merinda Park Learning and Community Centre
141–147 Endeavour Drive
Cranbourne North VIC 3977
Telephone: 03 5996 9056

Swinburne University
Croydon Campus
12-50 Norton Road
Croydon VIC 3136
Telephone: 03 9726 1656

AMES Dandenong
280 Thomas Street

Dandenong VIC 3175
Telephone: 03 8791 2401

NMIT Epping
Building A
Corner Dalton Road and Cooper Street
Epping VIC 3076
Telephone: 03 9269 1023

Fitzroy Learning Network Incorporated
198 Napier Street
Fitzroy VIC 3065
Telephone: 03 9417 2897

AMES Footscray
289 Barkly Street
Footscray VIC 3011
Telephone: 03 9687 3494

Diversitat
68-70 Little Ryrie Street
Geelong VIC 3220
Telephone: 03 5222 5947

Glenroy Neighbourhood Learning Centre
5B Cromwell Street
Glenroy VIC 3046
Telephone: 03 9304 3910

Holmesglen Institute of TAFE
Waverley Campus
595 Waverley Road
Glen Waverley VIC 3150
Telephone: 03 9564 1977

Bass Coast Adult Education Centre
239 White Road
Wonthaggi VIC 3995
Telephone: 03 5672 3115

Hampton Park Community House
16-20 Stuart Avenue
Hampton Park VIC 3976
Telephone: 03 9799 0708

Swinburne University
Hawthorn Campus
John Street
Hawthorn VIC 3122
Telephone: 03 9214 8634

Ballarat University
Horsham Campus
Baillie Street
Horsham VIC 3400
Telephone: 03 5362 2600

Victoria University
Werribee Campus
Hoppers Lane
Hoppers Crossing VIC 3030
Telephone: 03 9919 724

Bendigo TAFE (BRIT)
Kyneton Campus
43–47 Edgecombe Street
Kyneton VIC 3444
Telephone: 03 5422 2737

Meadow Heights Learning Shop
C/– Visy Care Learning Centre
3–13 Hudson Circuit
Meadow Heights VIC 3048
Telephone: 03 9301 9200

AMES Flagstaff
Level 3
255 William Street
Melbourne VIC 3000
Telephone: 03 9926 4717

Victoria University
Melton Campus
Rees Road
Melton South VIC 3338
Telephone: 03 9919 7521

Sunraysia Institute of TAFE
Mildura Campus
Benetook Avenue
Mildura VIC 3500
Telephone: 03 5022 3952

Central Gippsland Institute of TAFE
Moe Library
Kirk Street
Moe VIC 3825
Telephone: 03 5120 4503

Holmesglen Institute of TAFE
Moorabbin Campus
488 South Road
Moorabbin VIC 3189
Telephone: 03 9209 5768

Central Gippsland Institute of TAFE
Corner Princes Drive and Monash Way
Morwell VIC 3841
Telephone: 03 5120 4503

AMES Noble Park
60 Douglas Street
Noble Park VIC 3174
Telephone: 03 8558 8800

Diversitat 25–41 Arunga Avenue
Norlane
North Geelong VIC 3214
Telephone: 03 5260 6000

North Melbourne Language and Learning Incorporated
Ground Floor, 33 Alfred Street
North Melbourne VIC 3051
Telephone: 03 9326 7447

AMES Oakleigh
1A Palmerston Grove
Oakleigh VIC 3166
Telephone: 03 9563 477

Glen Eira Adult Learning Centre Incorporated
419 North Road
Ormond VIC 3204
Telephone: 03 9578 8996

Living and Learning Incorporated
6B Henry Street
Pakenham VIC 3810
Telephone: 03 5941 2389

NMIT Preston
Building T
Cramer Street
Preston VIC 3072
Telephone: 03 9269 8346

Swinburne University
Prahran Campus
Room PK412, Level 4
PK Building
St John Street
Prahran VIC 3181
Telephone: 03 9214 6985

Carringbush Adult Learning Education
Incorporated
415 Church Street
Richmond VIC 3121
Telephone: 03 9421 2392

Carringbush Adult Learning Education
Incorporated
9 Belgium Avenue
Richmond VIC 3121
Telephone: 03 9421 2392

Preston Reservoir Adult Community Education (PRACE)
C/- Merrilands Community Centre
Corner Asquith and Strudee Streets
Reservoir VIC 3073
Telephone: 03 9462 6077

Sunraysia Institute of TAFE
Robinvale Campus
160 Bromley Road
Robinvale VIC 3549
Telephone: 03 5051 8300

Goulburn Ovens Institute of TAFE (GO TAFE)
Shepparton Campus
Fryers Street
Shepparton VIC 3630
Telephone: 03 5833 2760

AMES Springvale
Corner Boulton Street and Springvale Road
Springvale VIC 3171
Telephone: 03 9546 0099

Ballarat University
Stawell Campus
Sloane Street
Stawell VIC 3380
Telephone: 03 5327 8091

AMES St Albans
16 Victoria Square
Victoria Crescent

St Albans VIC 3021
Telephone: 03 9366 0433

Victoria University Sunshine Campus
460 Ballarat Road
Sunshine VIC 3020
Telephone: 03 9919 7244

Sunraysia Institute of TAFE
Swan Hill Campus
64 Sea Lake Road
Swan Hill VIC 3585
Telephone: 03 5036 0216

Traralgon Neighbourhood Learning House
11-13 Breed Street
Traralgon VIC 3844
Telephone: 03 5120 4503

Central Gippsland Institute of TAFE
Corner Lidiard & Lansdowne Streets
Traralgon VIC 3844
Telephone: 03 5120 4564

Swinburne University
Wantirna Campus
369 Stud Road
Wantirna VIC 3152
Telephone: 03 9210 1175

Community College Gippsland
71 Korumburra–Warragul Road
Warragul VIC 3820
Telephone: 03 5622 6000

South West TAFE
Warrnambool Campus
Timor Street
Warrnambool VIC 3280
Telephone: 03 5564 8911

AMES Werribee
Suite 7 & 8, Level 1
75-79 Watton Street
Werribee VIC 3030
Telephone: 03 8744 0011

Wodonga TAFE
87 McKay Street
West Wodonga VIC 3690
Telephone: 02 6055 634

Western Australia AMEP Learning Centre Locations

Great Southern Institute of Technology
Anson Road
Albany WA 6330
Telephone: 1800 862 166

Polytechnic West Armadale AMEP
145 Jull Street
Armadale WA 6112
Telephone: 08 9497 7084

Kimberly Training Institute
68 Cable Beach Road
Broome WA 6725
Telephone: 1800 862 166

South West Institute of Technology
Robertson Drive
Bunbury WA 6230
Telephone: 1800 862 166

South West Institute of Technology
Busselton Campus
2–12 South Street
Brusselton WA 6280
Telephone: 1800 862 166

Polytechnic West Carlisle AMEP
Corner Bank and Oats Street
Carlisle WA 6101
Telephone: 08 9267 7335

MMRC Clarkson
237A Ocean Keys Road
Clarkson WA 6030
Telephone: 1800 862 166

Westerly Family Centre
27 Westerly Way
Cooloongup WA 6168
Telephone: 1800 862 166

East Fremantle Baptist Church
239 Canning Highway
East Fremantle WA 6158
Telephone: 1800 862 166

Polytechnic West CBD AMEP
170 Wellington Street
East Perth WA 6004
Telephone: 08 6330 455

Durack Institute of Technology
Geraldton Campus
Fitzgerald Street
Geraldton WA 6530
Telephone: 1800 862 166

Joondalup Lotteries House
12/ 70 Davidson Terrace

Joondalup WA 6027
Telephone: 1300 202 134

Great Southern Institute of Technology
Katanning Campus
9 Dore Street
Katanning WA 6317
Telephone: 1800 862 166

Boogurlarri Community Centre
82 Langford Avenue
Langford WA 6147
Telephone: 1800 862 166

Central Institute of Technology
B Block
Richmond Street
Leederville WA 6007
Telephone: 1300 202 134

Mandurah Baptist Church
370 Pinjarra Road
Mandurah WA 6210
Telephone: 1800 862 166

Community Resource Centre
The Old Hospital
33 Tunbridge Street
Margaret River WA 6285
Telephone: 1800 862 166

AMEP Mirrabooka
22-24 Chesterfield Road
Mirrabooka
Mirrabooka WA 6061
Telephone: 08 9349 4806

Sunbury Community House
Cnr Sunbury and Chesterfield Road

Mirrabooka WA 6061
Telephone: 1300 202 134

Morley YMCA
Corner Wellington and Mangini Streets
Morley WA 6062
Telephone: 1300 202 134

Chung Wah Association
128 James Street
Northbridge WA 6003
Telephone: 1800 862 166

Central Institute of Technology
AMEP, Level 3
25 Aberdeen Street

Northbridge WA 6865
Telephone: 1300 202 134

Pilbara Institute
Hamilton Road
Port Hedland WA 6721
Telephone: 1800 862 166

All Nations Presbyterian Church
82 Beaufort Street
Perth WA 6000
Telephone: 1800 862 166

Polytechnic West Thornlie AMEP
Burslem Drive
Thornlie WA 6108
Telephone: 08 9267 7609

Acknowledgements

I wish to thank my wife, Joan, for her hard work, Sylvie Blair for all her suggestions and efforts on my behalf, and all my friends for listening patiently.

References

The Law Institutes of Victoria and New South Wales, Centrelink. Various Government bodies who supplied information, particularly:

The Department of Defence

The Department of Social Security

The Department of Immigration

The Department of Employment, Education and Training.

Robert Half Placement Agencies

The Australian Taxation Office

The Real Estate institutes of Victoria and New South Wales

Domain Group

Department of Health and Human Services

Index

Lightning Source UK Ltd.
Milton Keynes UK
UKOW04f0020100118
315840UK00018B/431/P